Fairy
Coloring Book

Illustrations by Henry Justice Ford

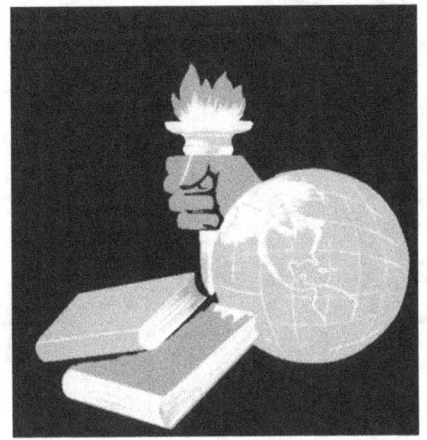

Hawaiian Heritage Press

ISBN-13: 978-1-943476-36-7

Henry Justice Ford (1860–1941) was an English artist
and illustrator, best known for his illustrations of Andrew Lang's
Fairy Books. Andrew Lang (1844–1912) was a poet, novelist,
and literary critic. It was thanks to Lang, Lang's wife Leonore
Blanche Alleyne, and other translators that many international
folk tales saw their first appearance in English. This coloring
book contains high-resolution reproductions of H.J. Ford's
gorgeous and sensual illustrations from Lang's Pink Fairy Book
(1904) and Grey Fairy Book (1905).

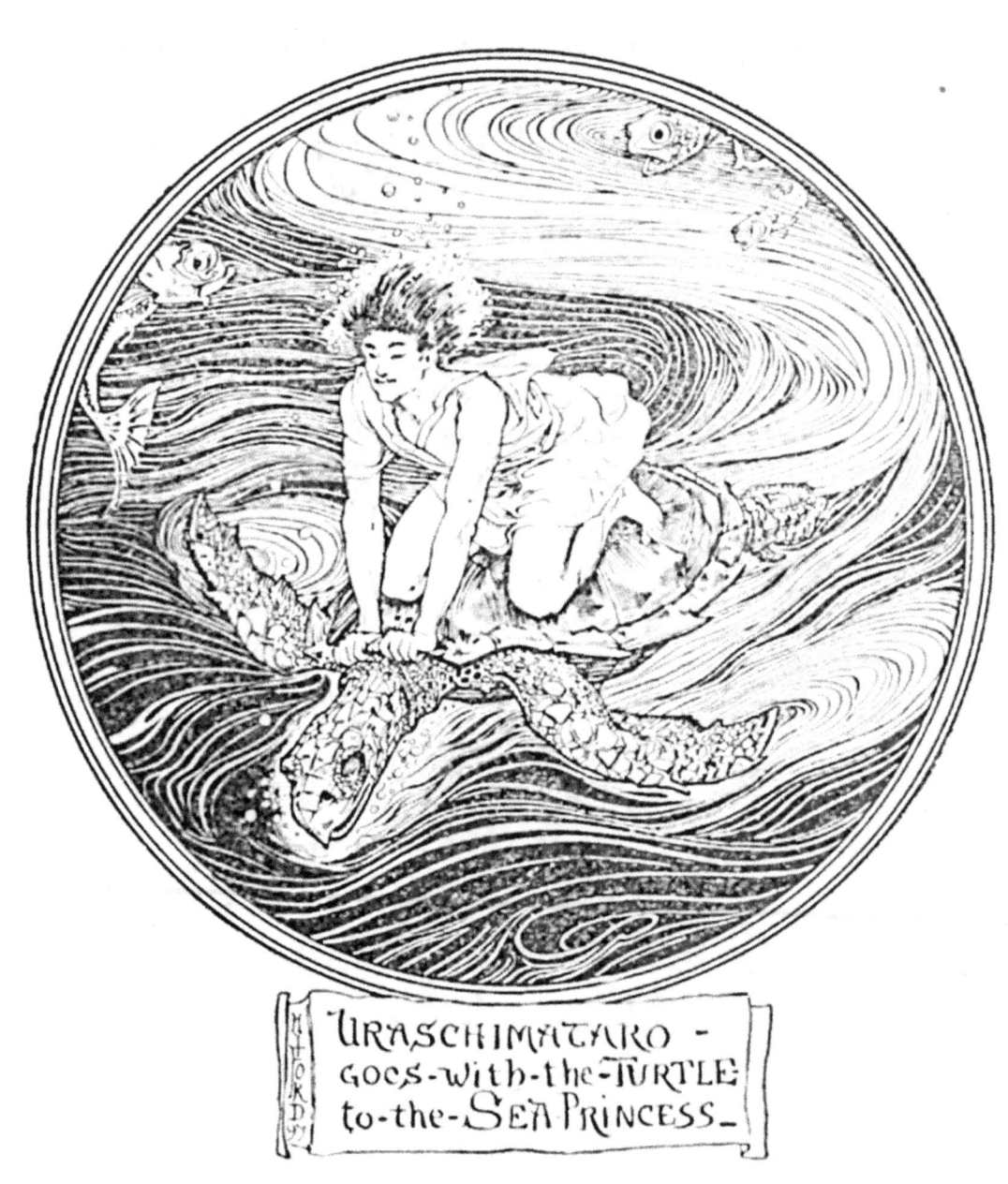

URASCHIMATARO -
Goes-with-the-TURTLE
to-the-SEA PRINCESS-

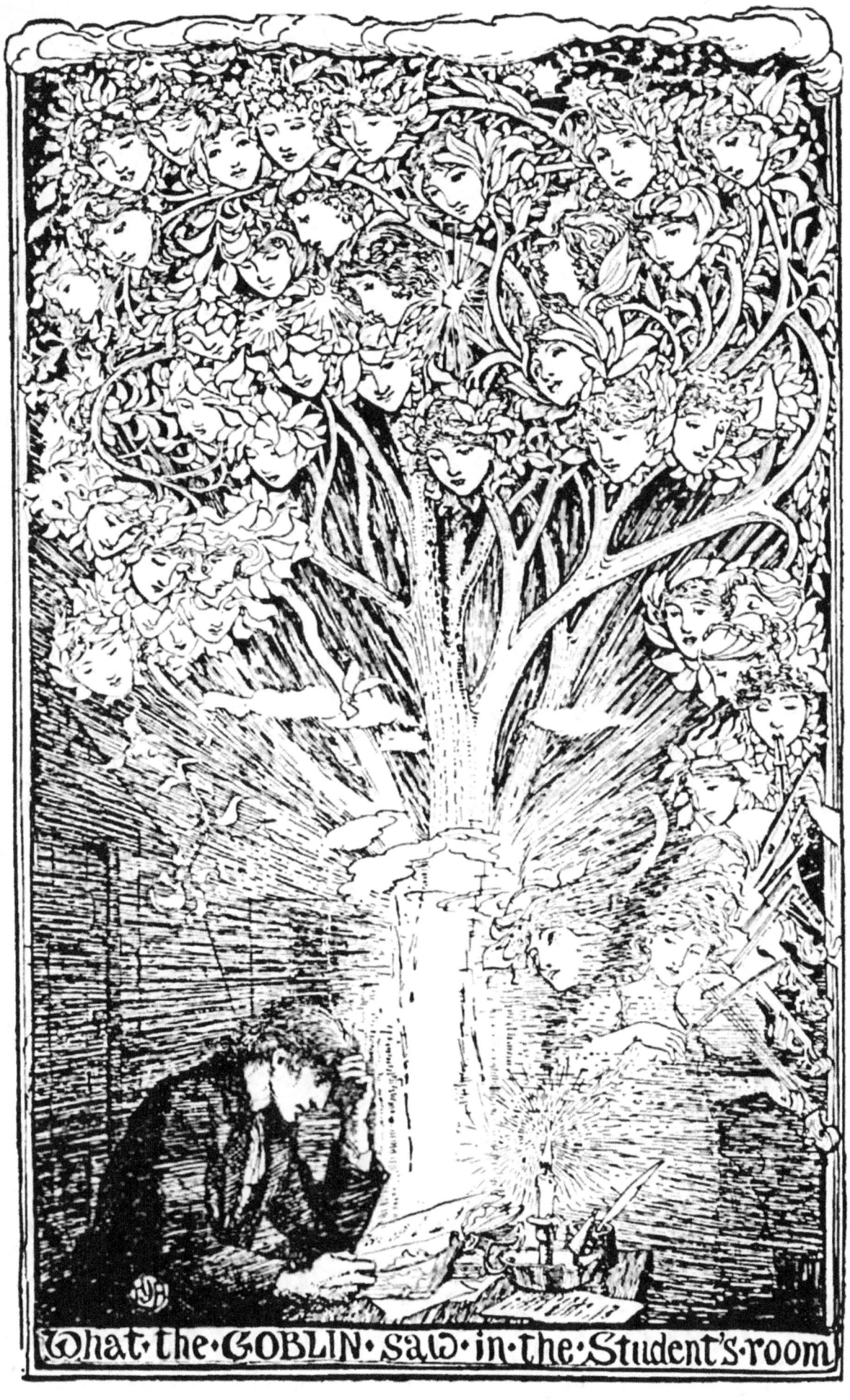

What the GOBLIN saw in the Student's room

Name:

Date:

Notes:

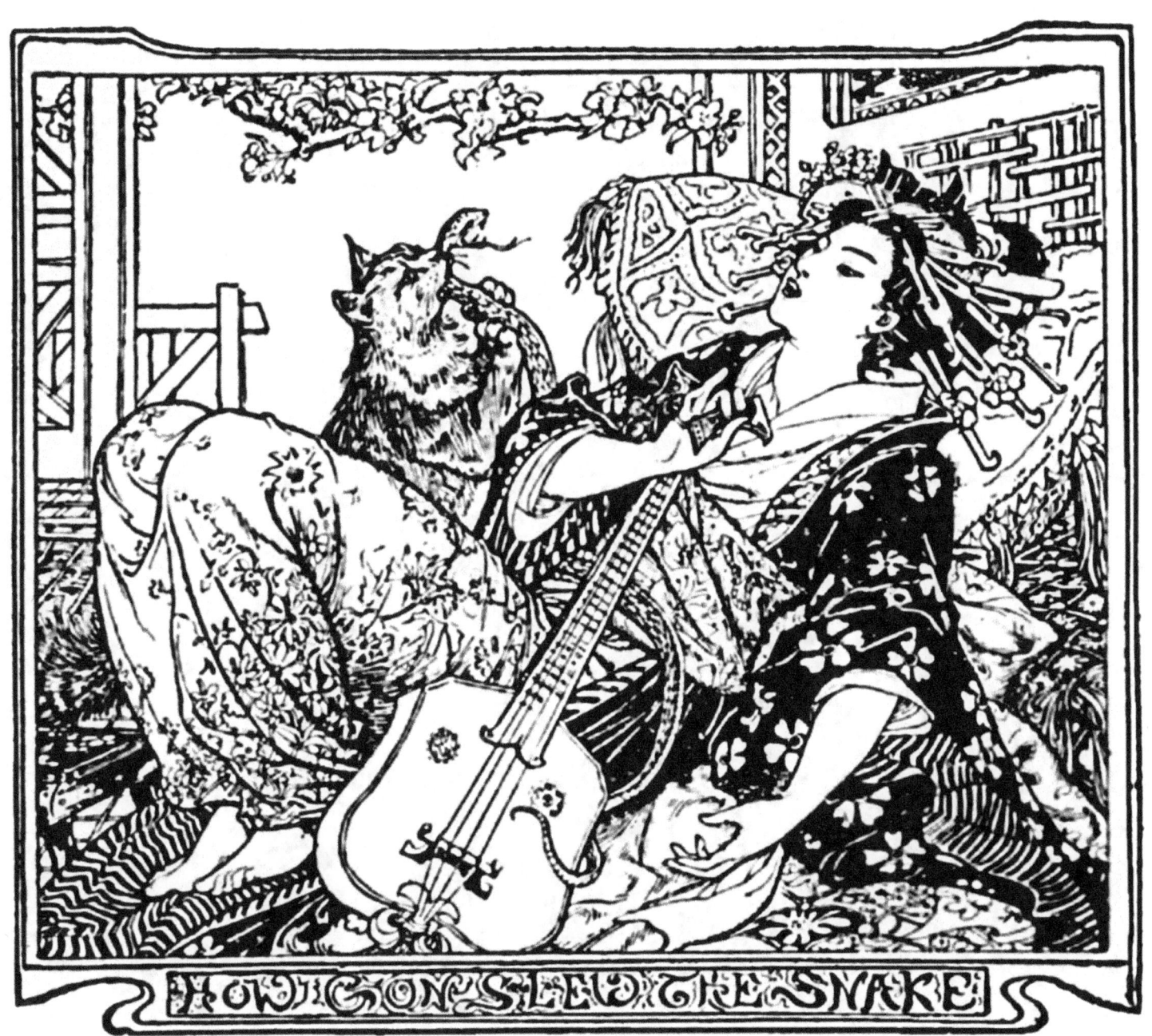

HOW IGON SLEW THE SNAKE

Name:

Date:

Notes:

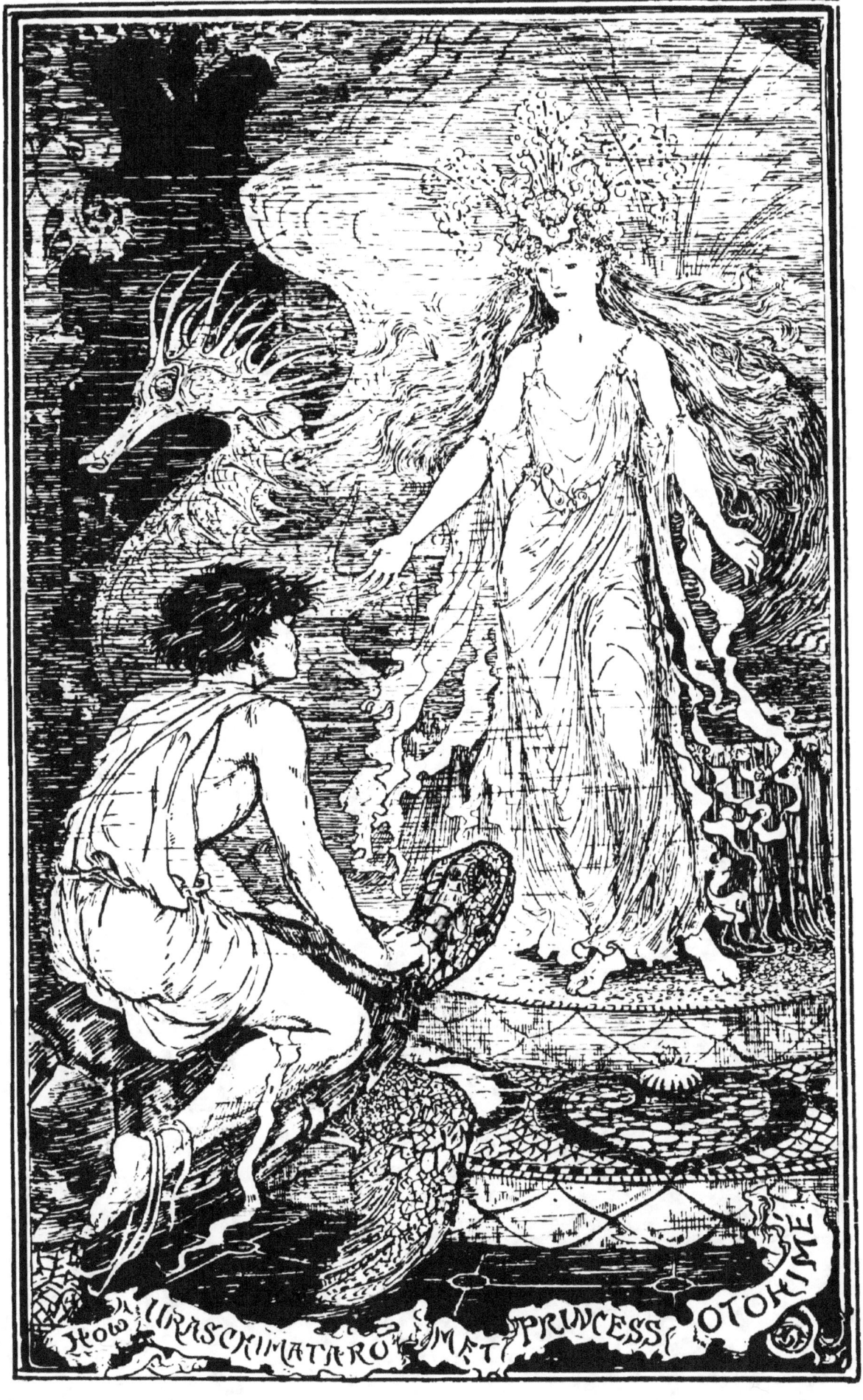

HOW URASCHIMATARO MET PRINCESS OTOHIME

Name:

Date:

Notes:

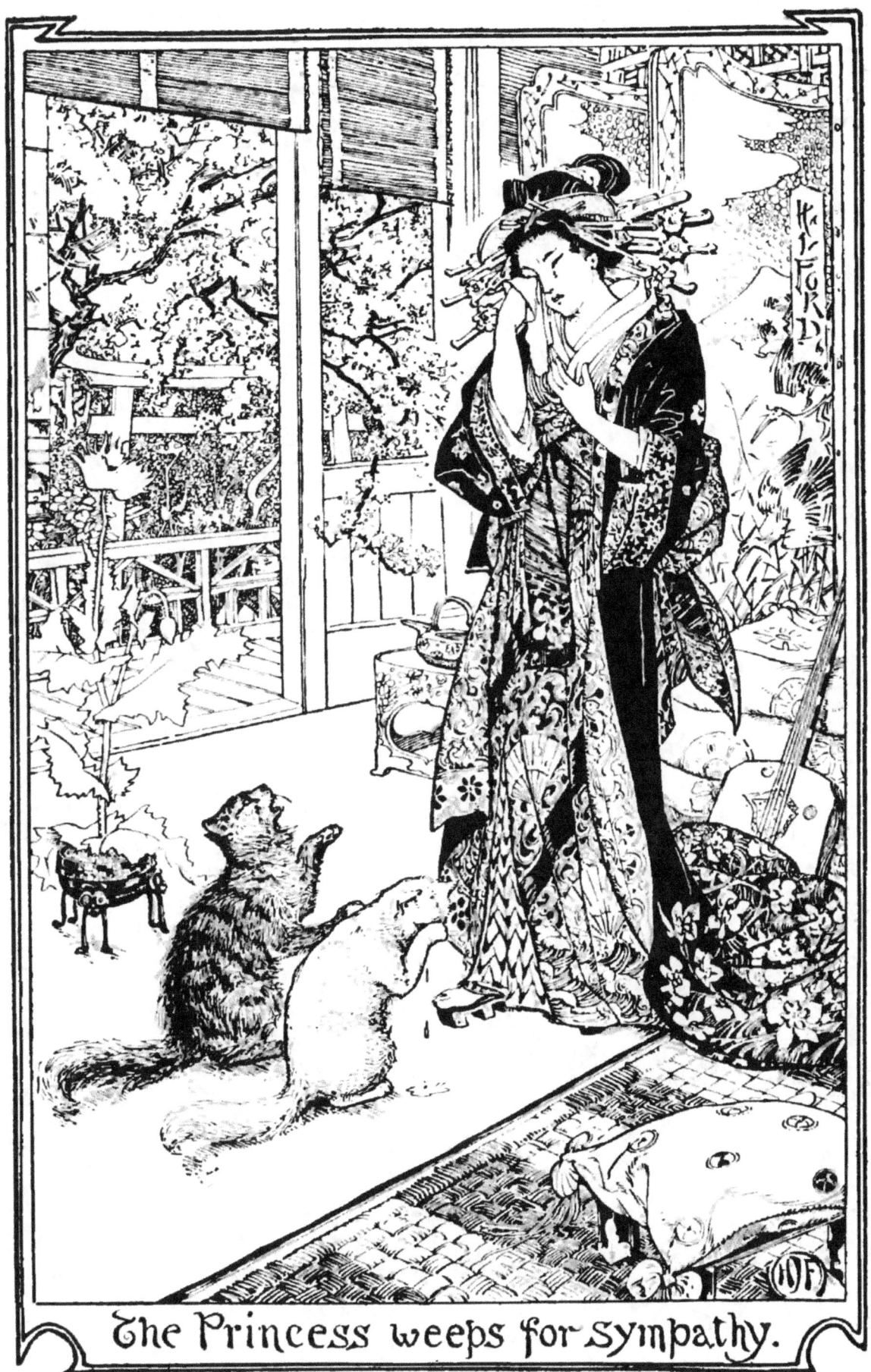

The Princess weeps for Sympathy.

Name:

Date:

Notes:

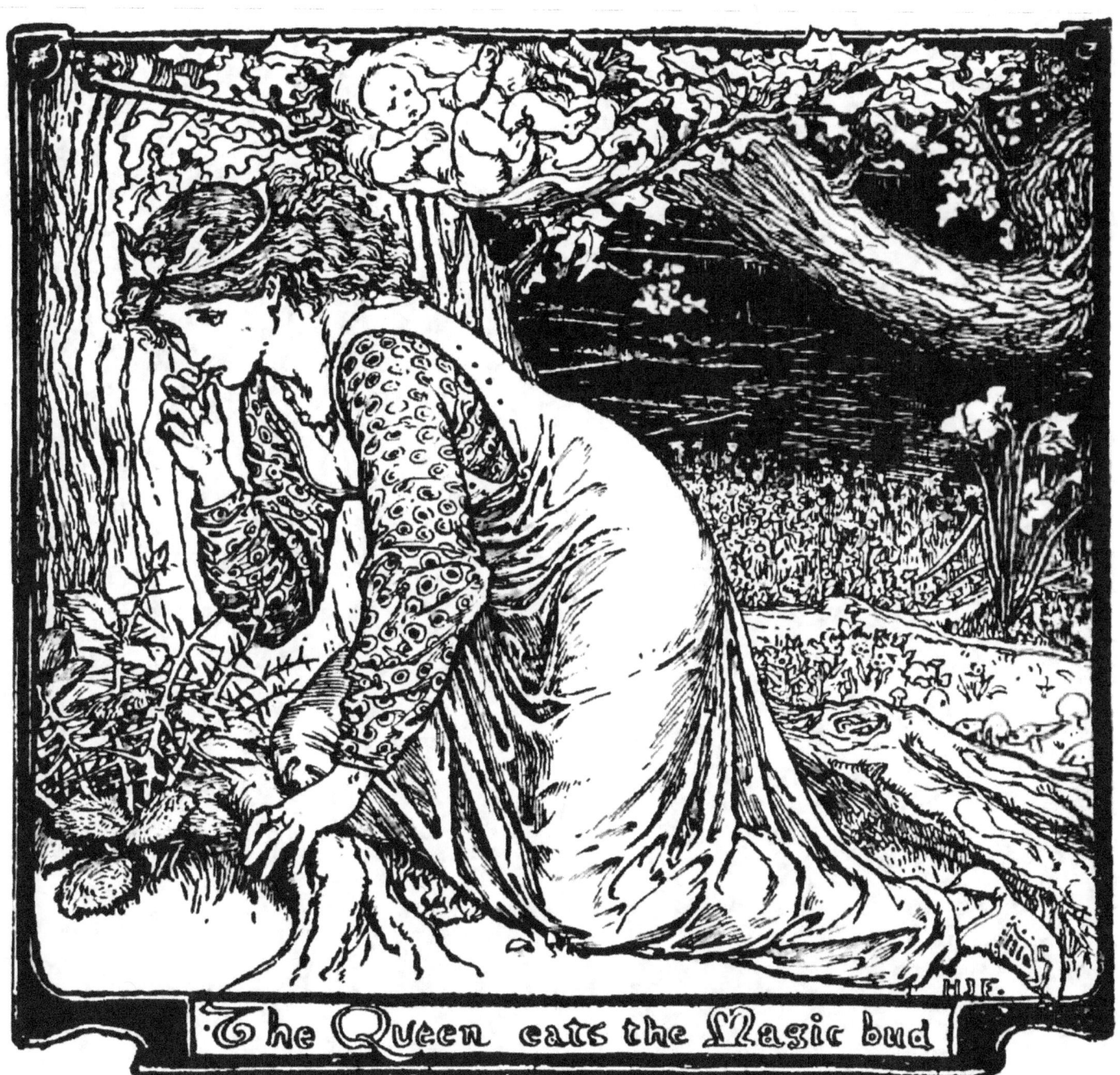

·The Queen eats the Magic bud

Name:

Date:

Notes:

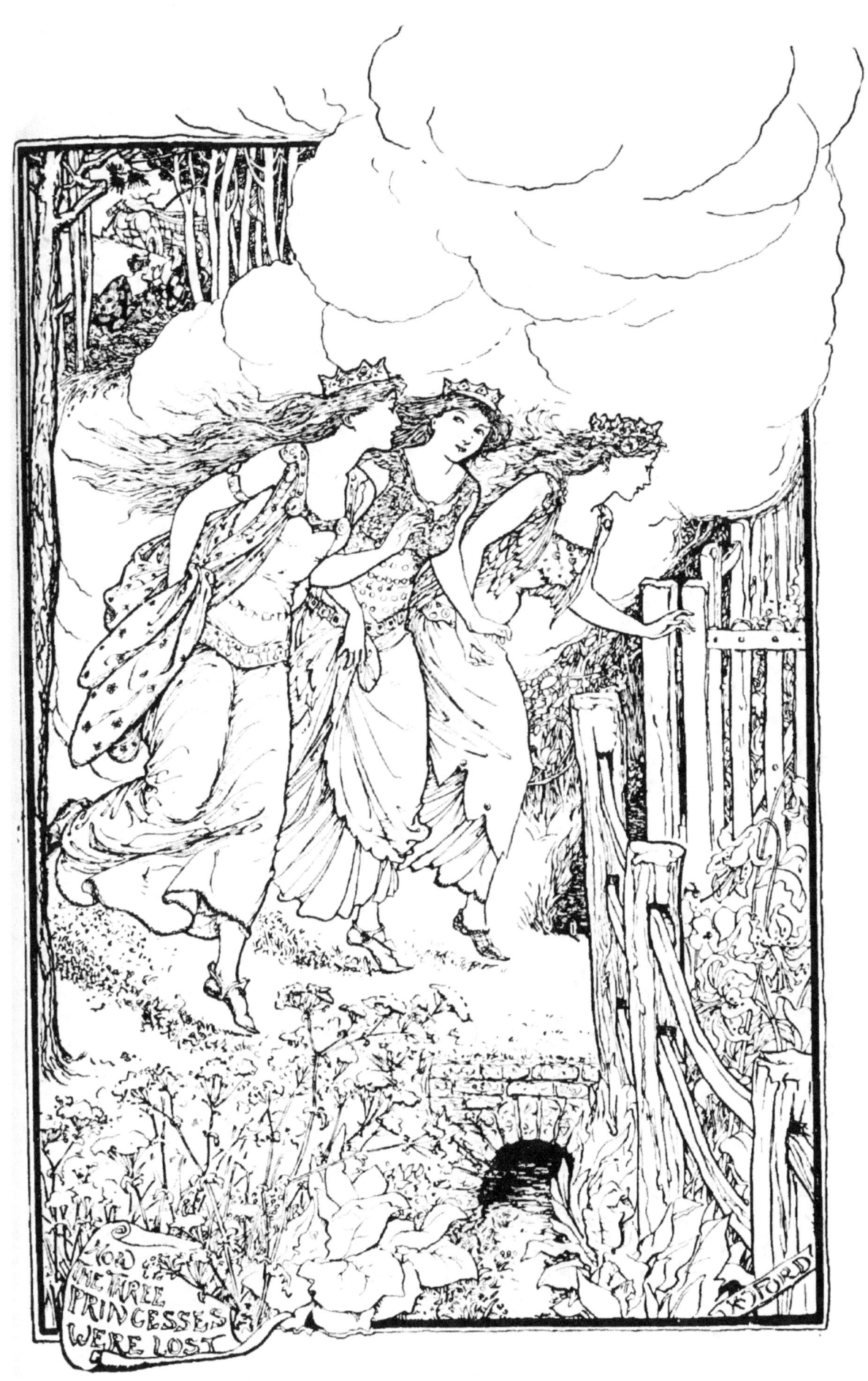

HOW THE THREE PRINCESSES WERE LOST

Name:

Date:

Notes:

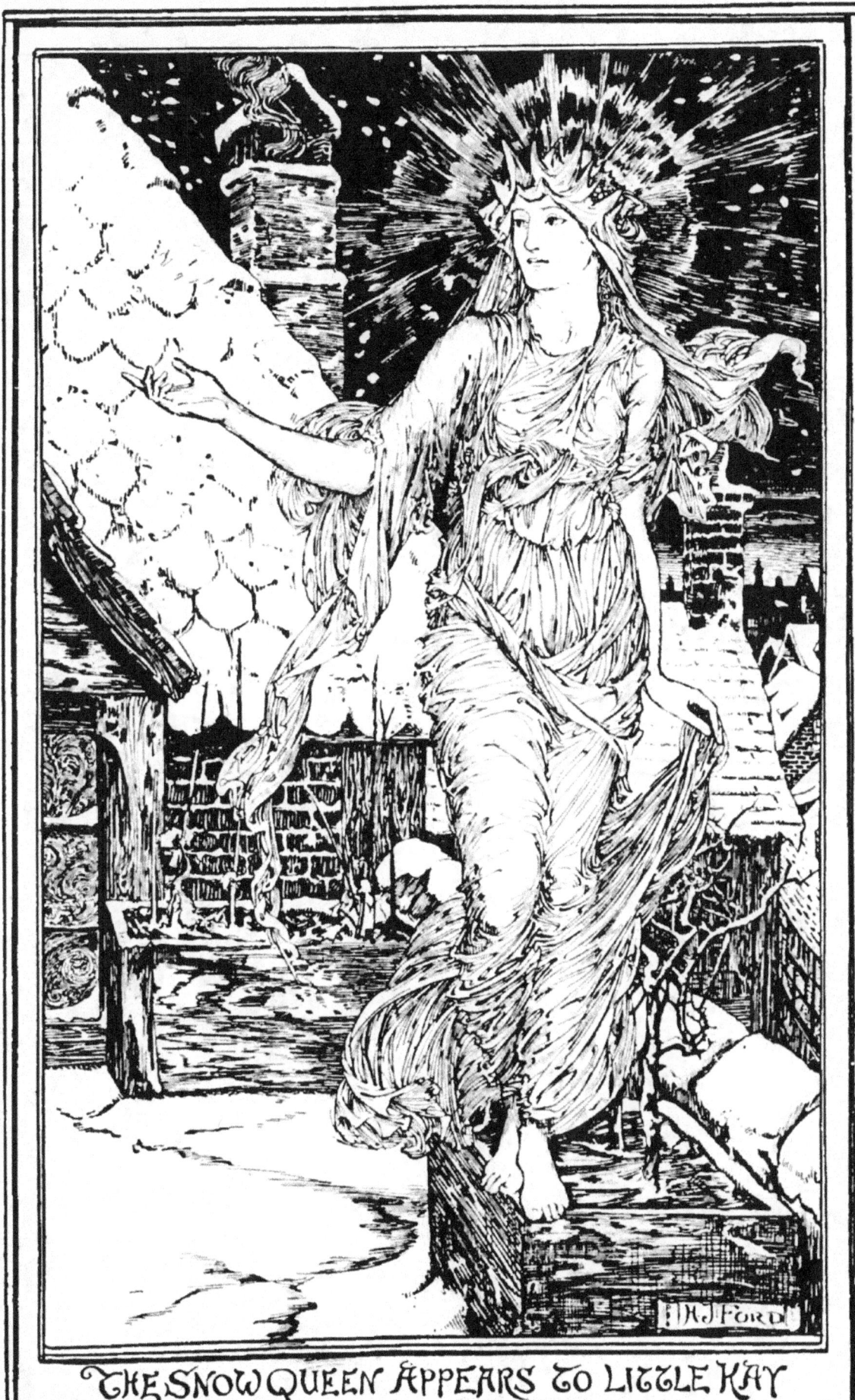

THE SNOW QUEEN APPEARS TO LITTLE KAY

Name:

Date:

Notes:

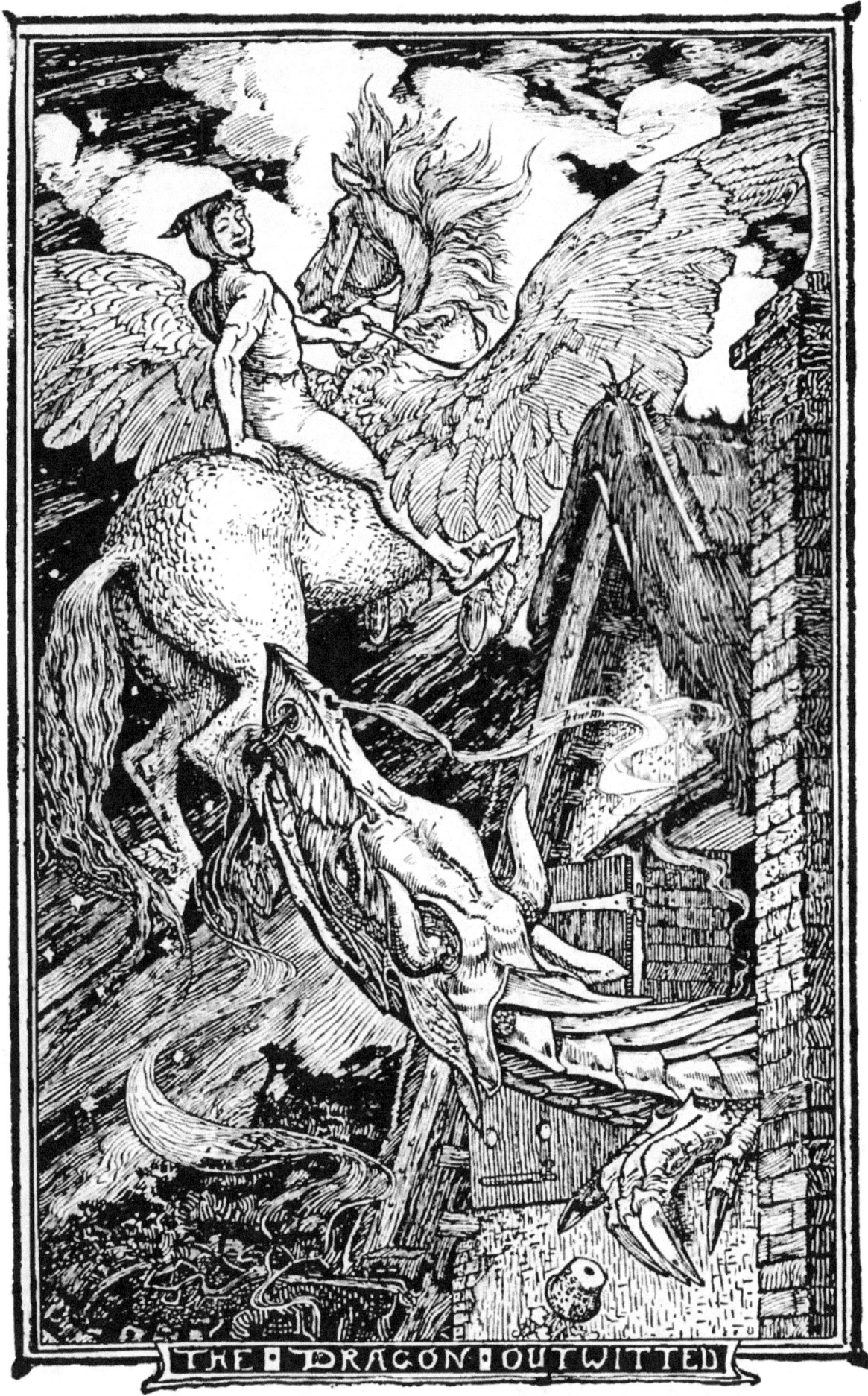

THE · DRAGON · OUTWITTED

Name:

Date:

Notes:

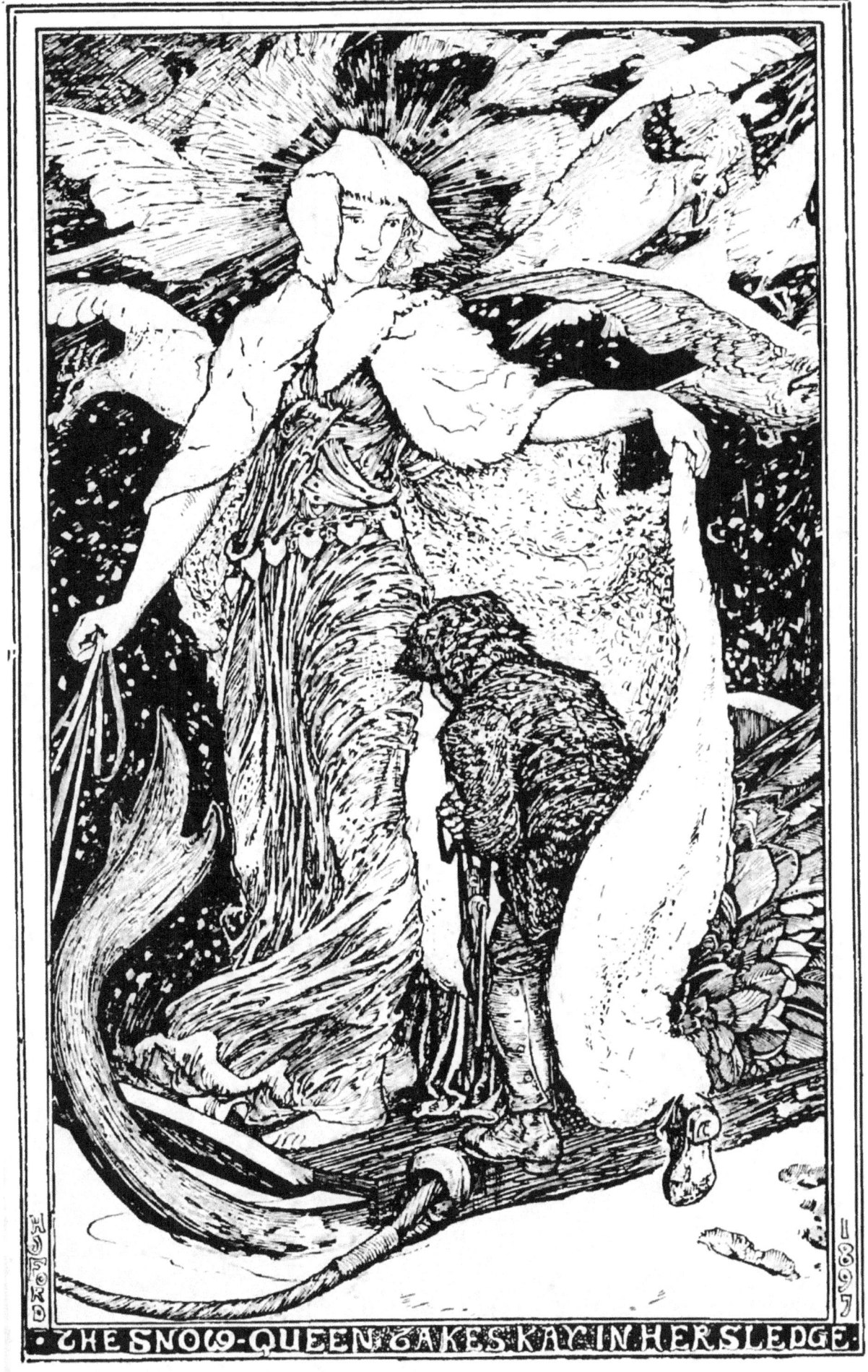

THE SNOW-QUEEN TAKES KAY IN HER SLEDGE

Name:

Date:

Notes:

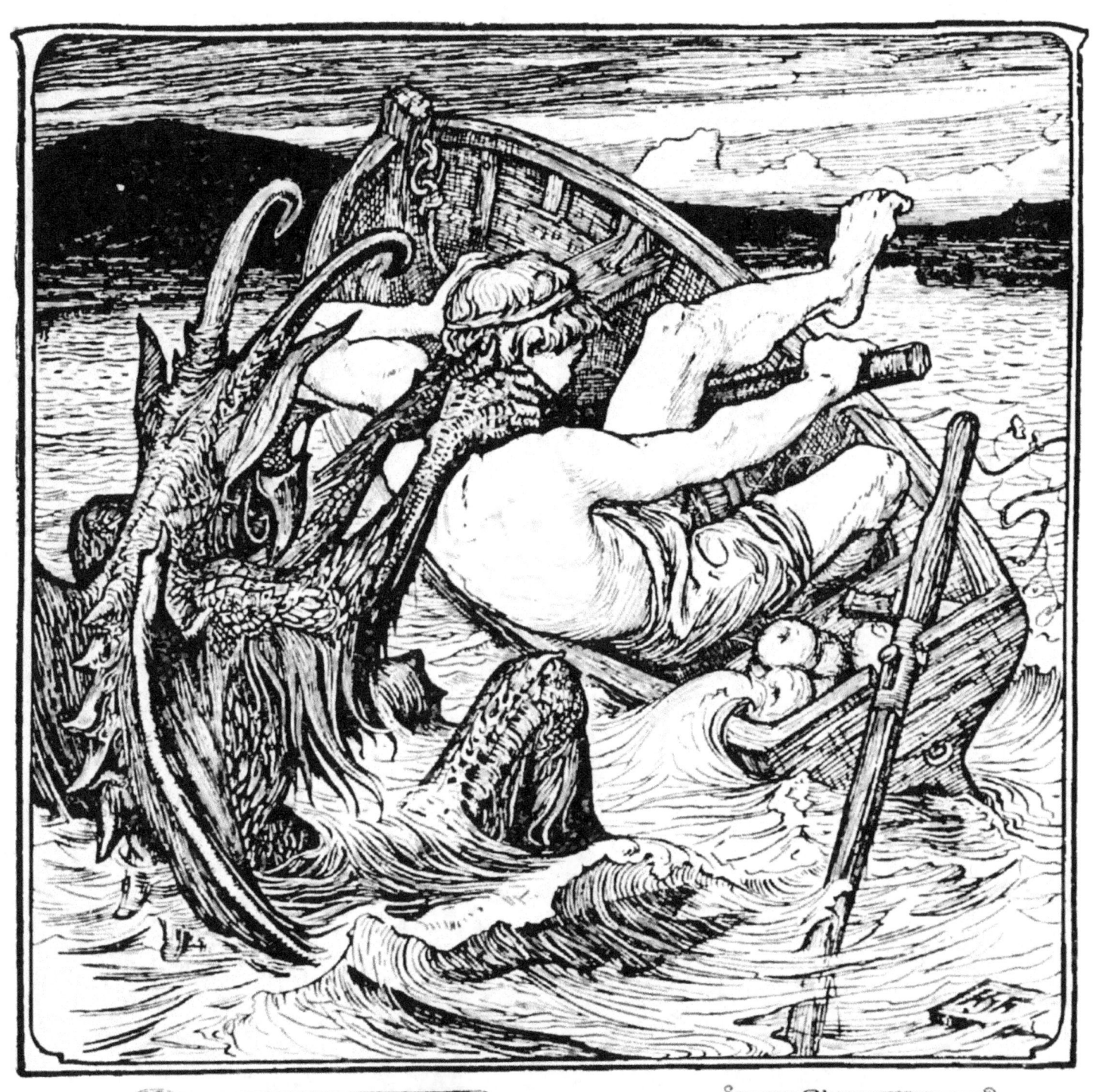

OLD ERIC CATCHES HANS

Name:

Date:

Notes:

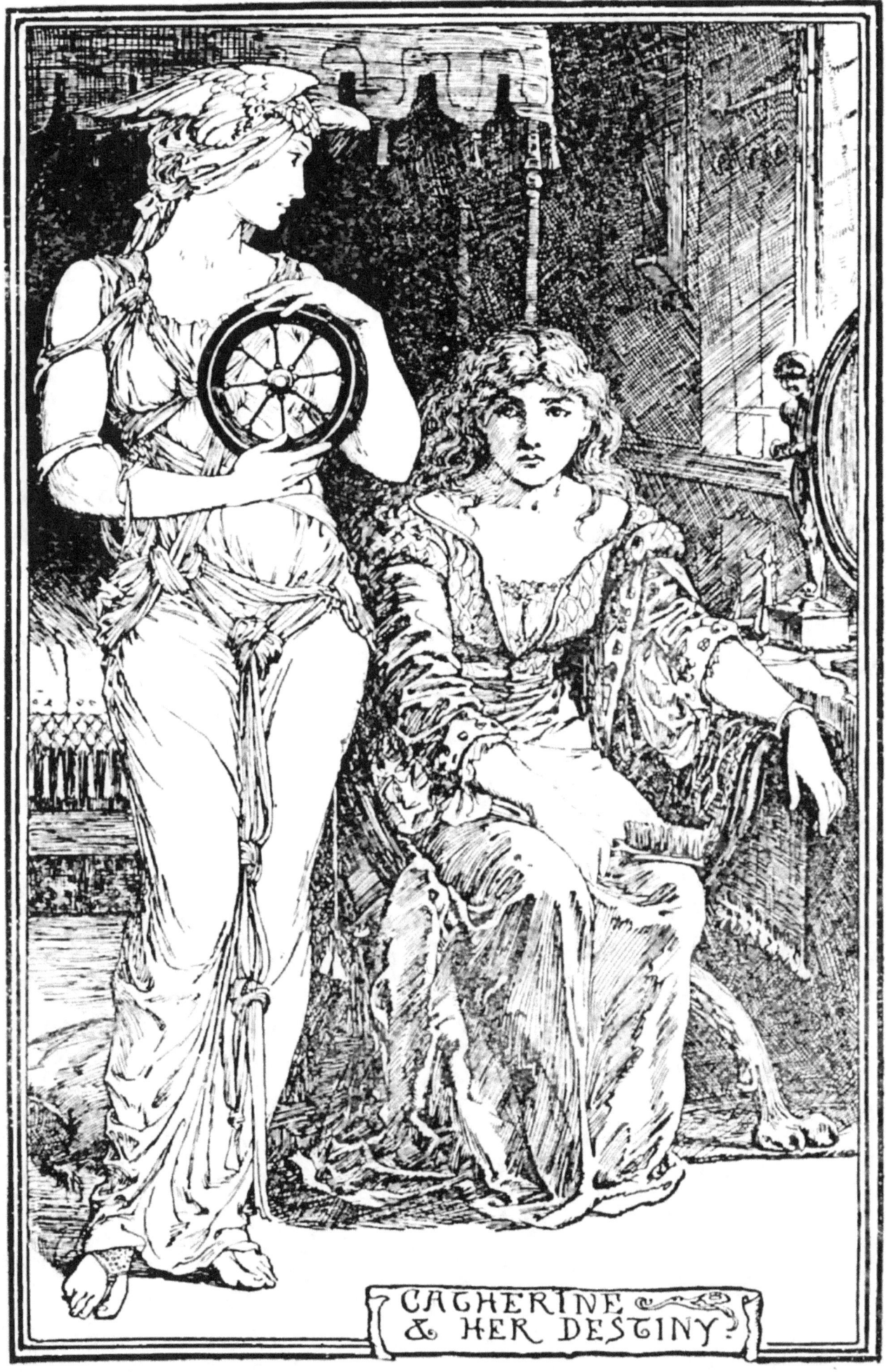

CATHERINE & HER DESTINY.

Name:

Date:

Notes:

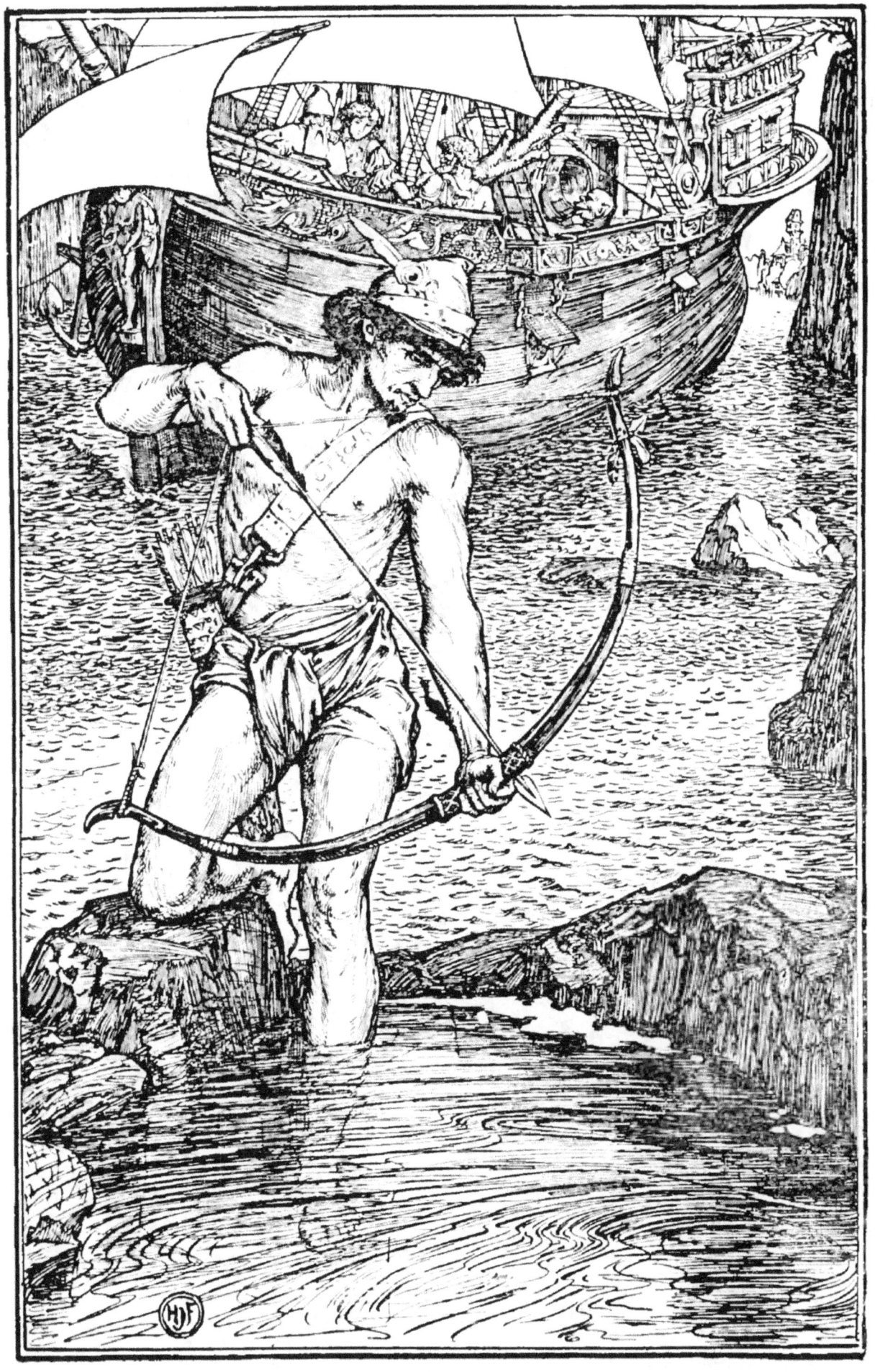

Name:

Date:

Notes:

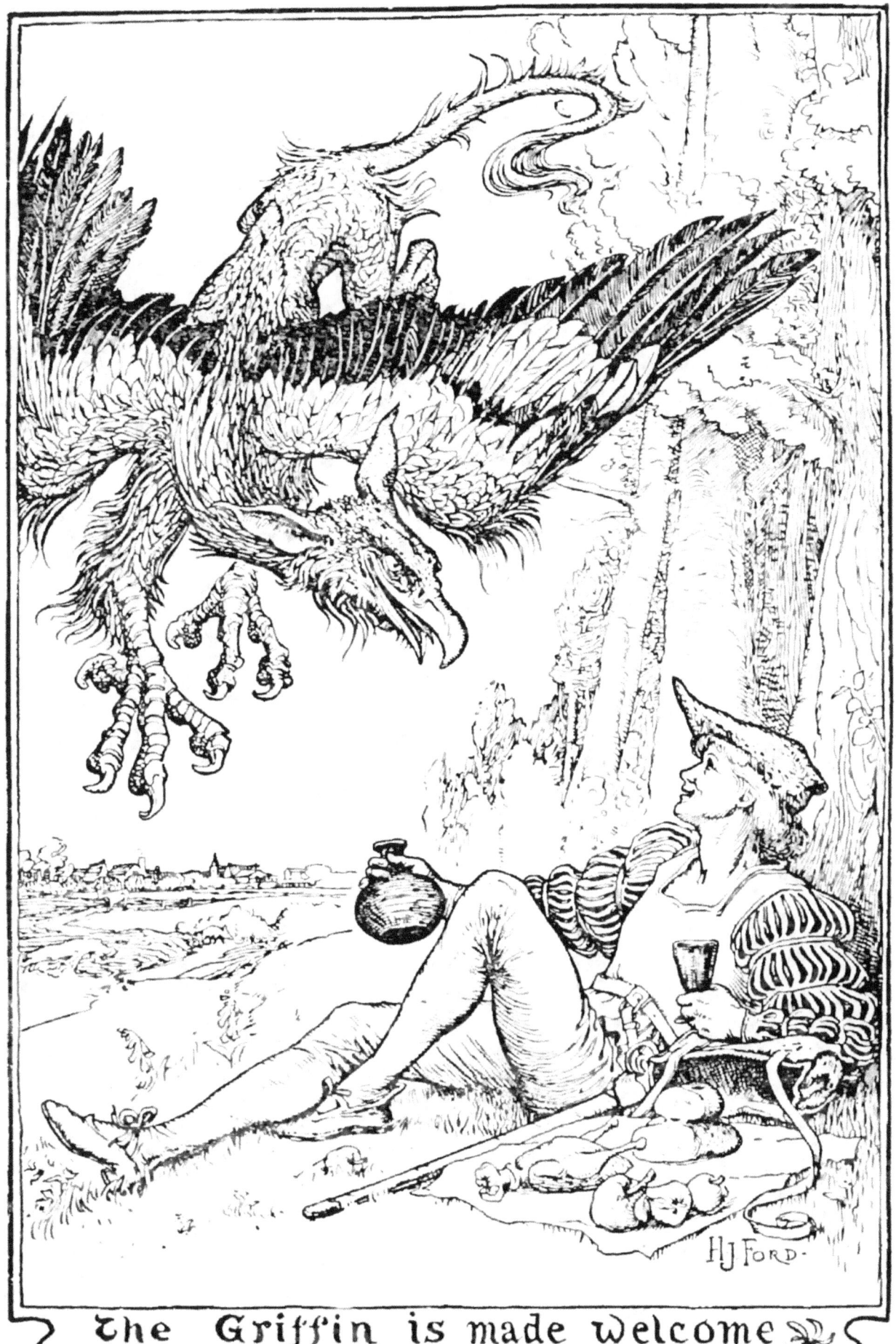

The Griffin is made Welcome

Name:

Date:

Notes:

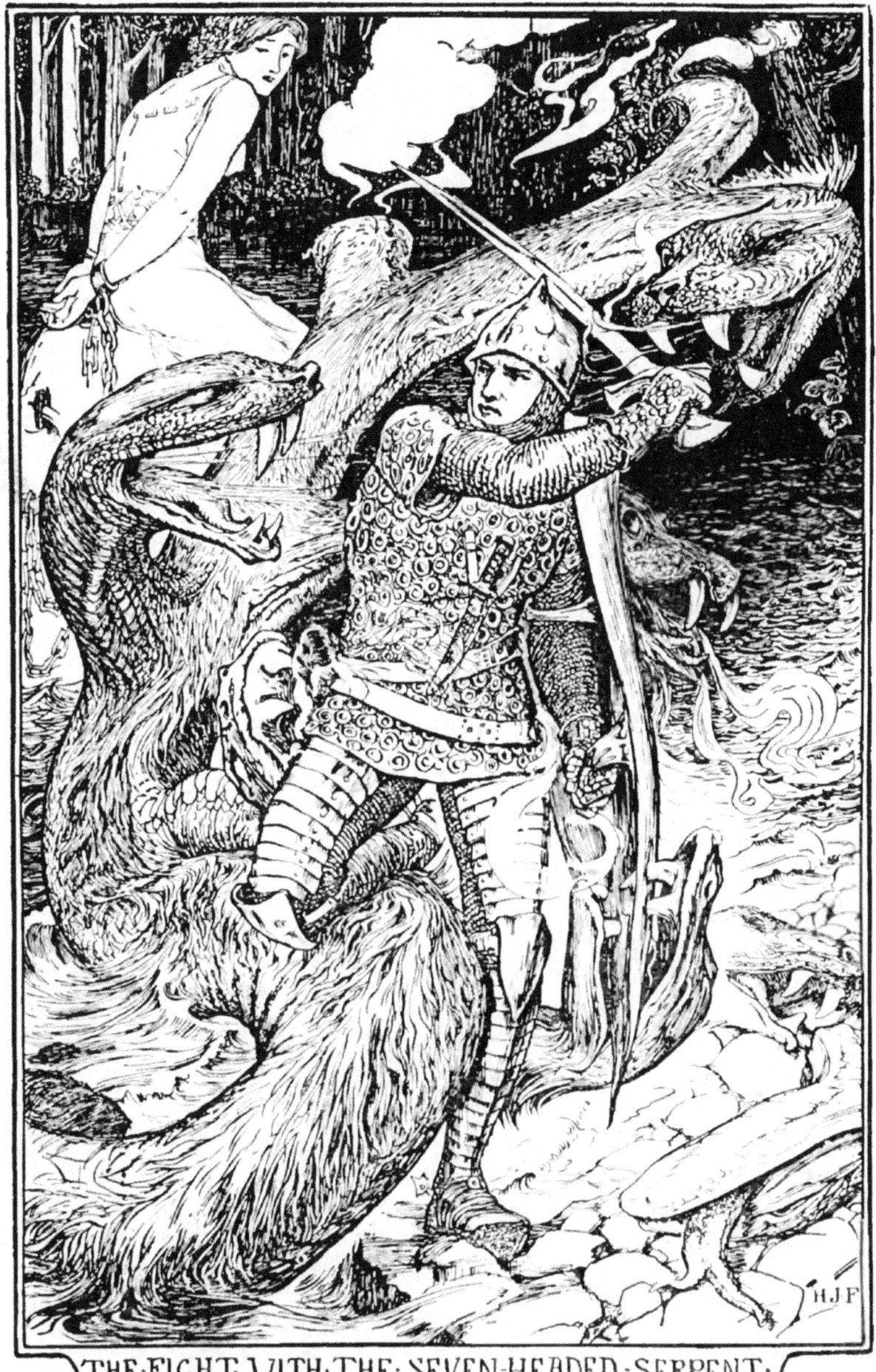

THE·FIGHT·WITH·THE·SEVEN·HEADED·SERPENT·

Name:

Date:

Notes:

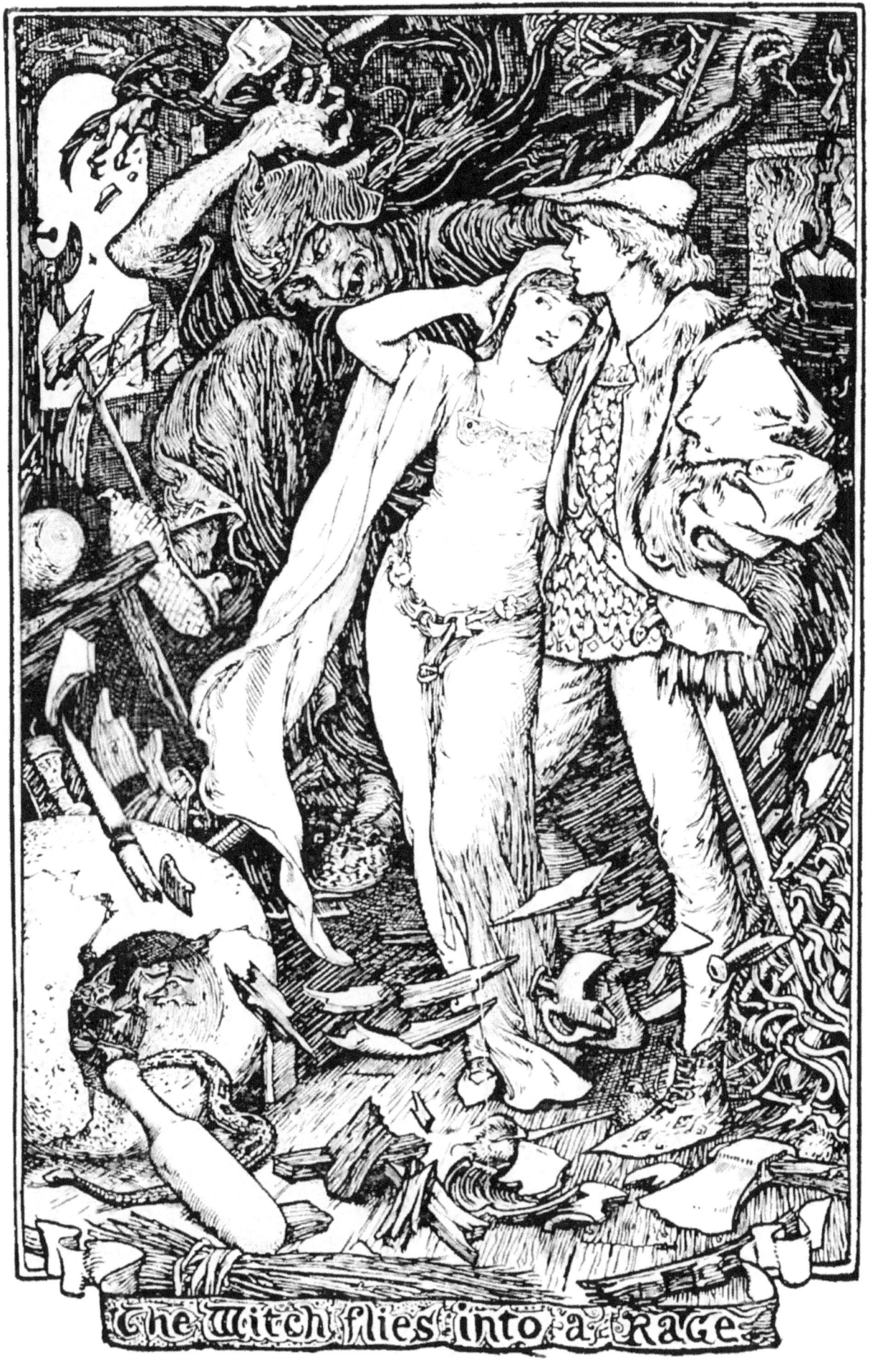

The Witch flies into a rage.

Name:

Date:

Notes:

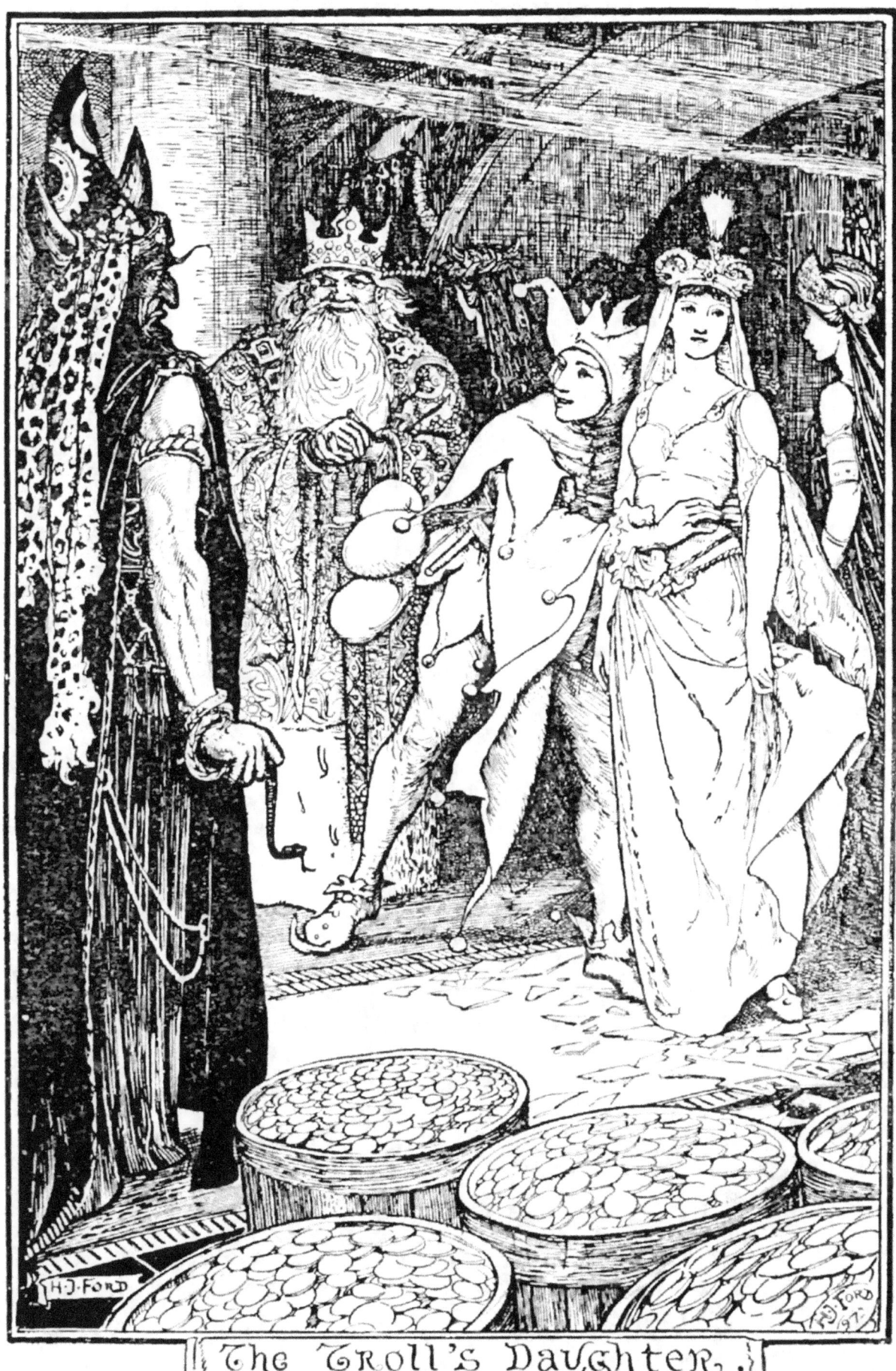

The Troll's Daughter.

Name:

Date:

Notes:

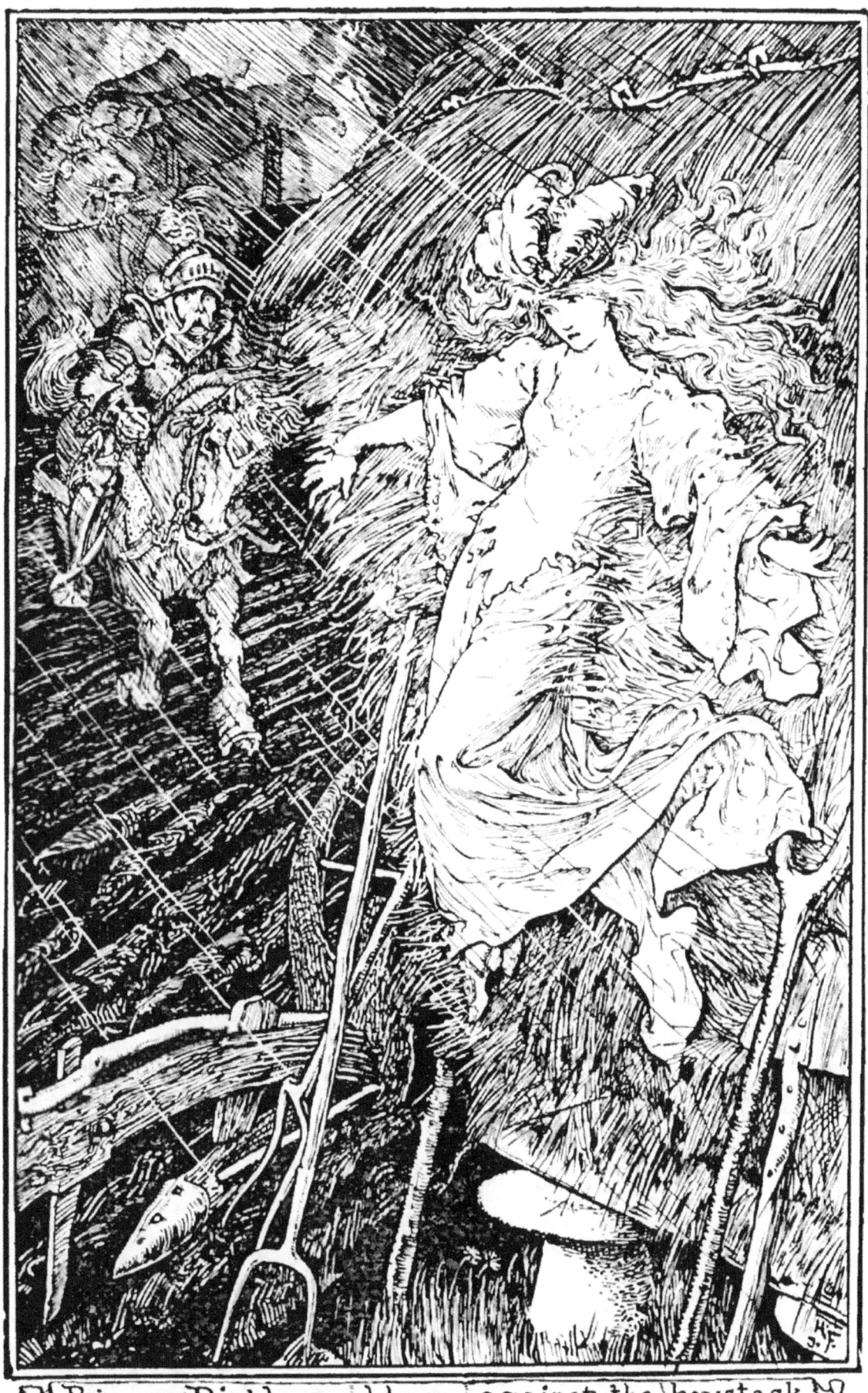

Princess Diaphana blown against the haystack

Name:

Date:

Notes:

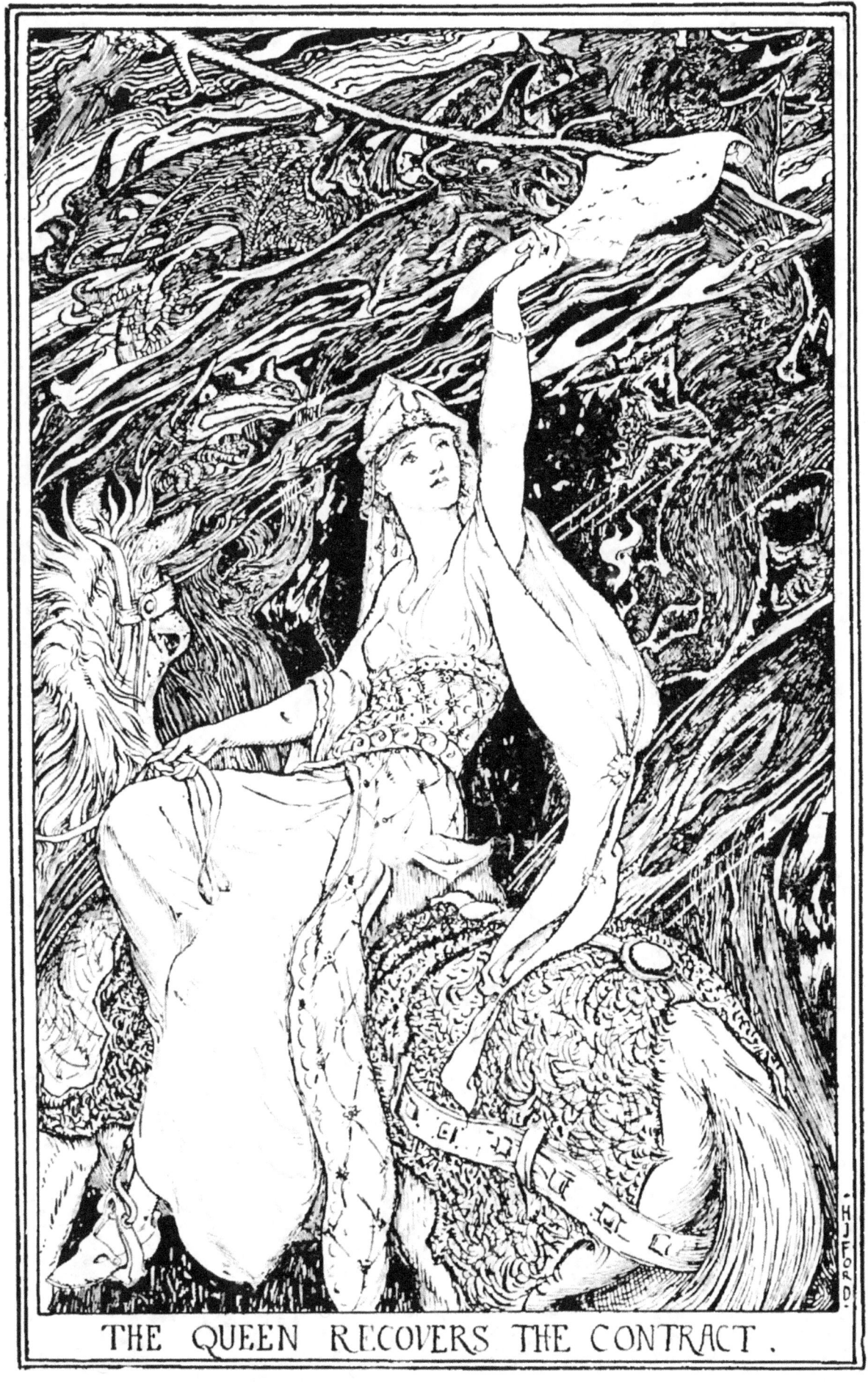

THE QUEEN RECOVERS THE CONTRACT.

Name:

Date:

Notes:

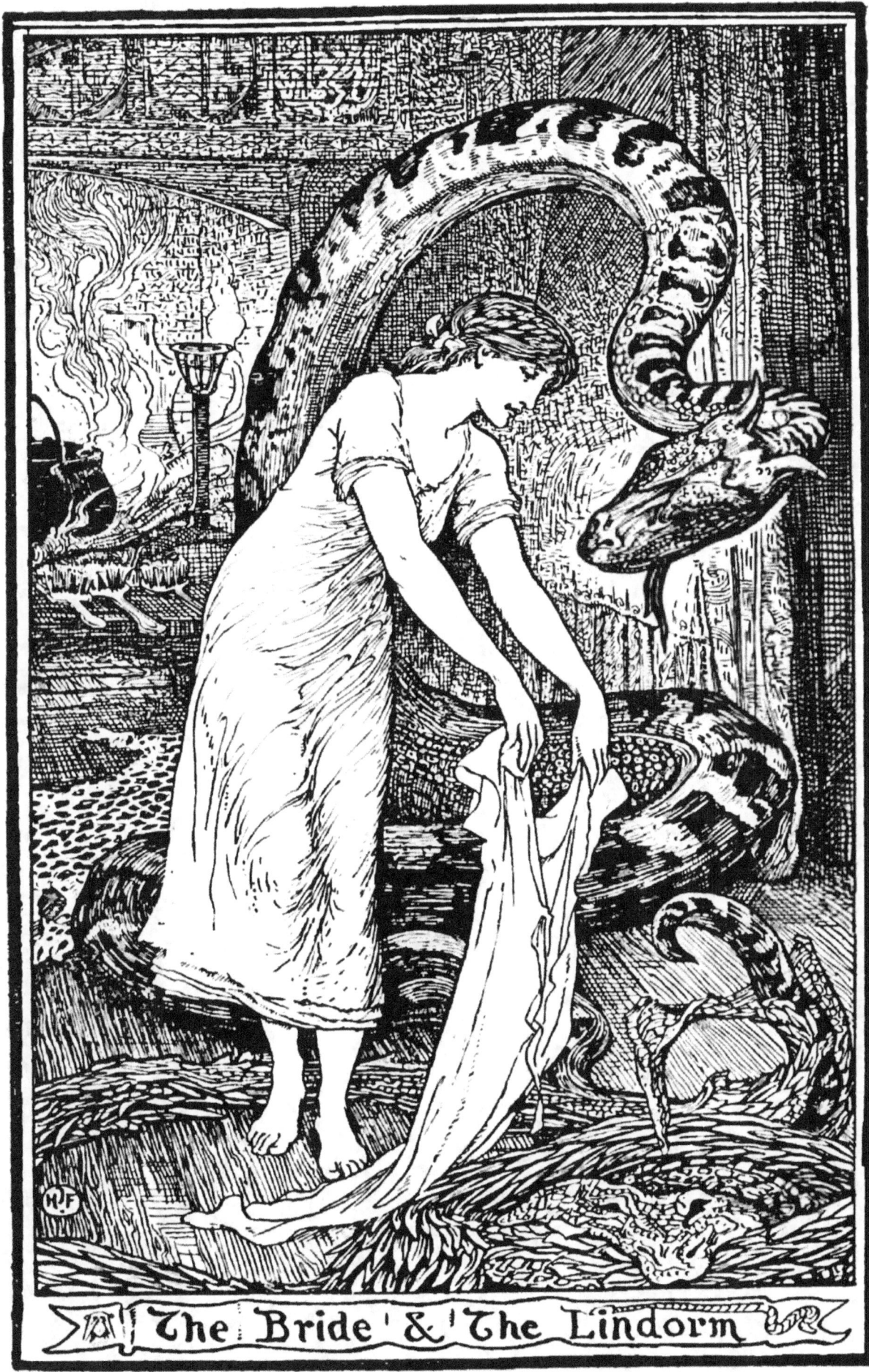

The Bride & The Lindorm

Name:

Date:

Notes:

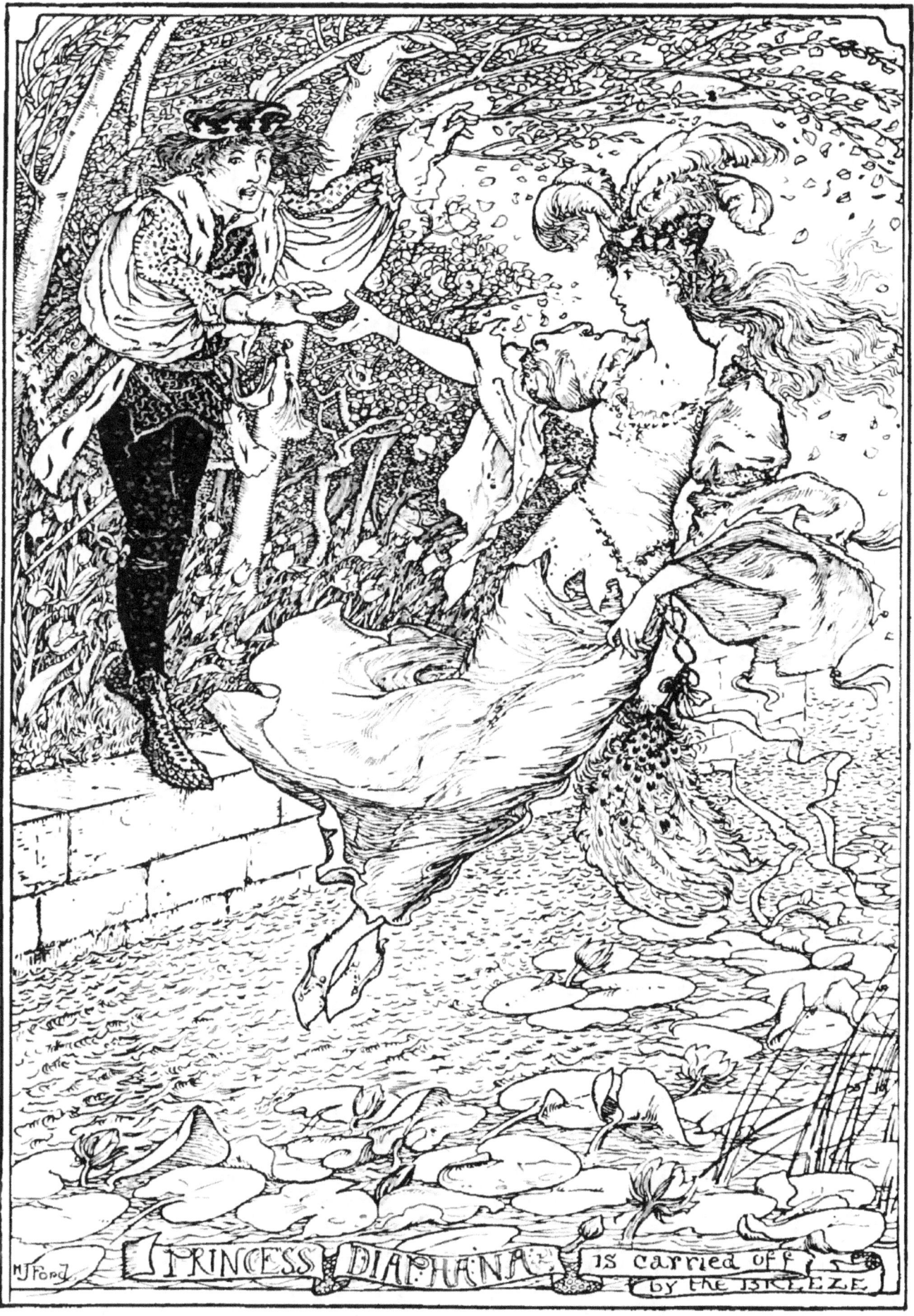

PRINCESS DIAPHANA is carried off by the BREEZE

Name:

Date:

Notes:

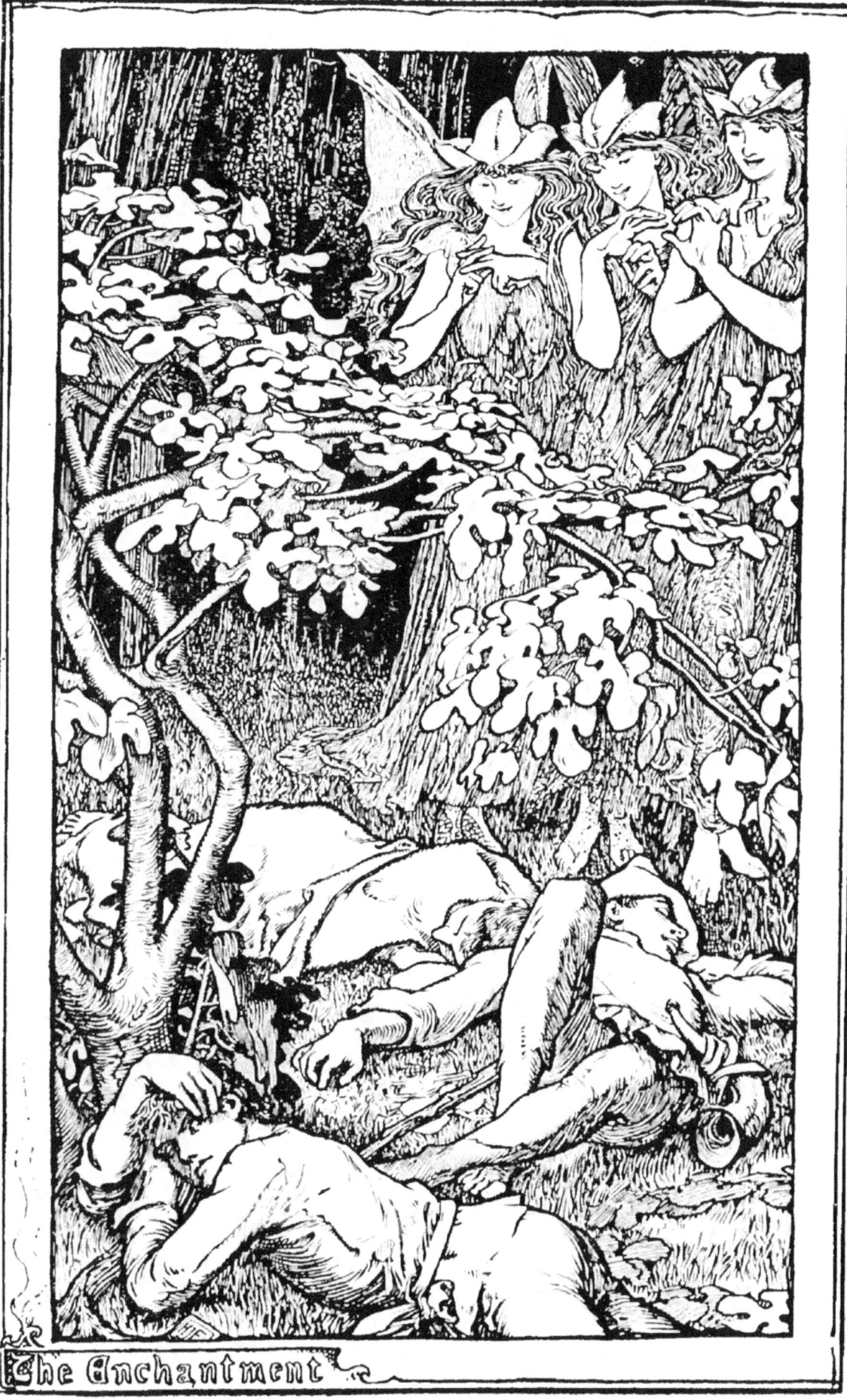

The Enchantment

Name:

Date:

Notes:

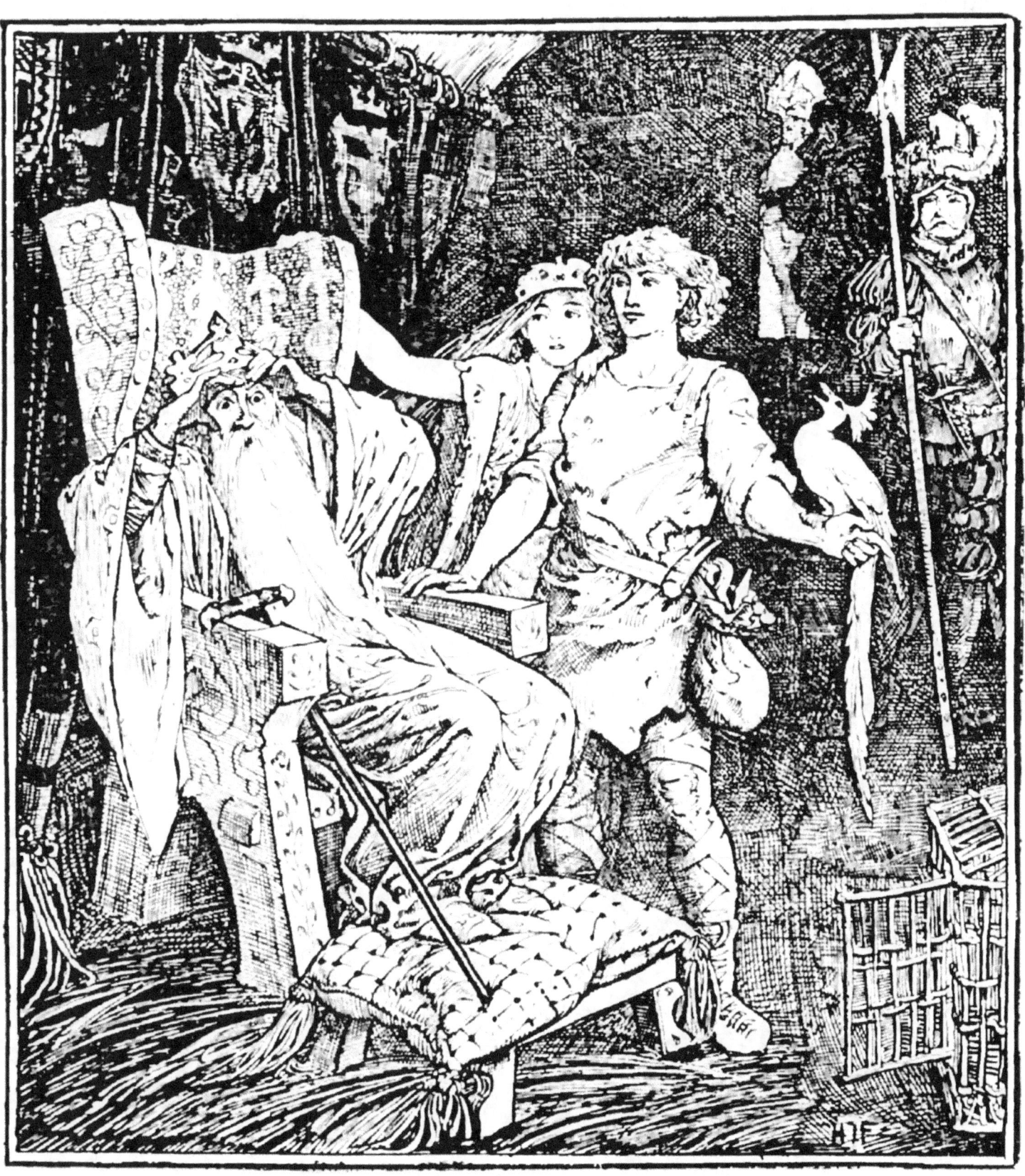

Name:
Date:
Notes:

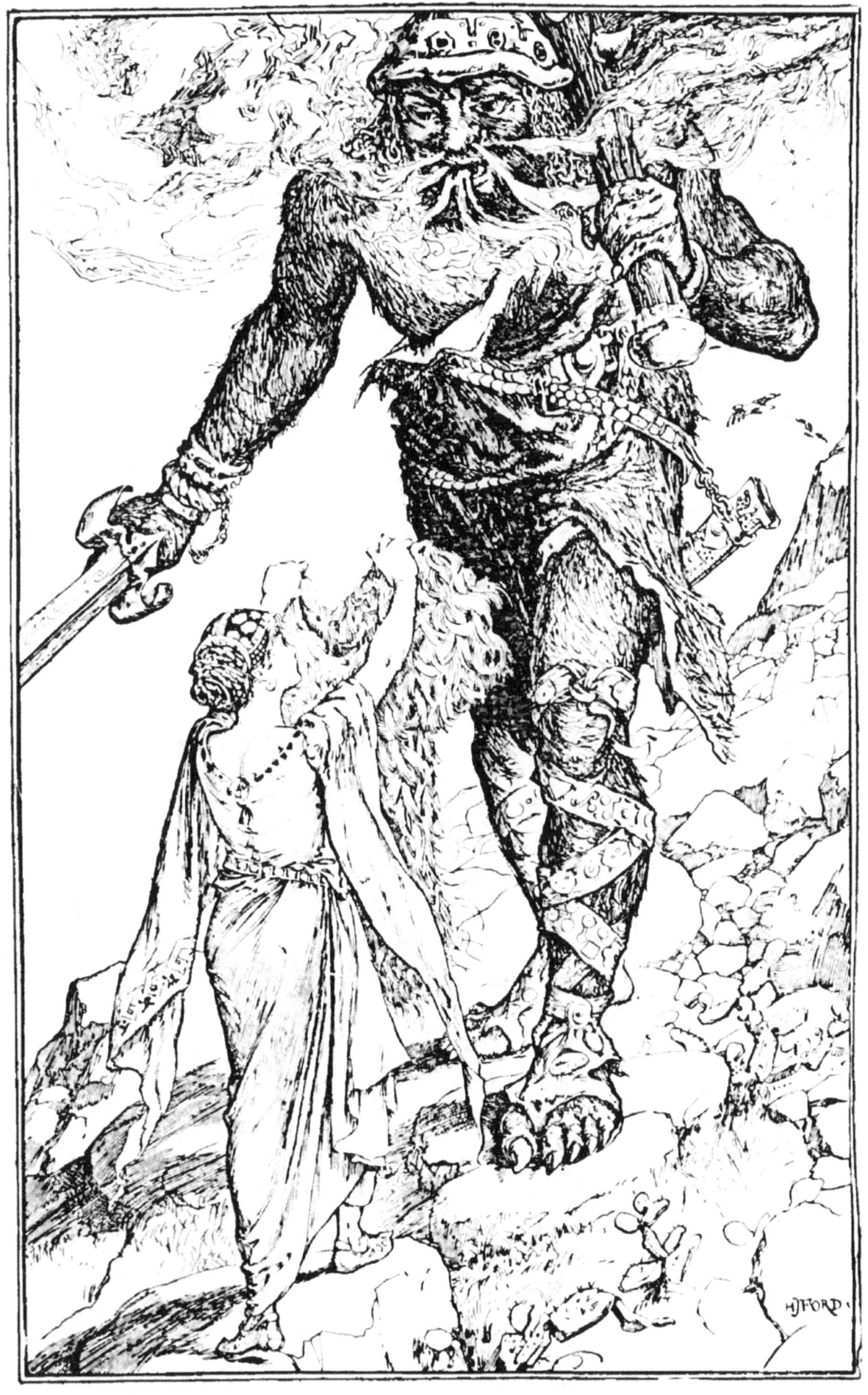

Name:
Date:
Notes:

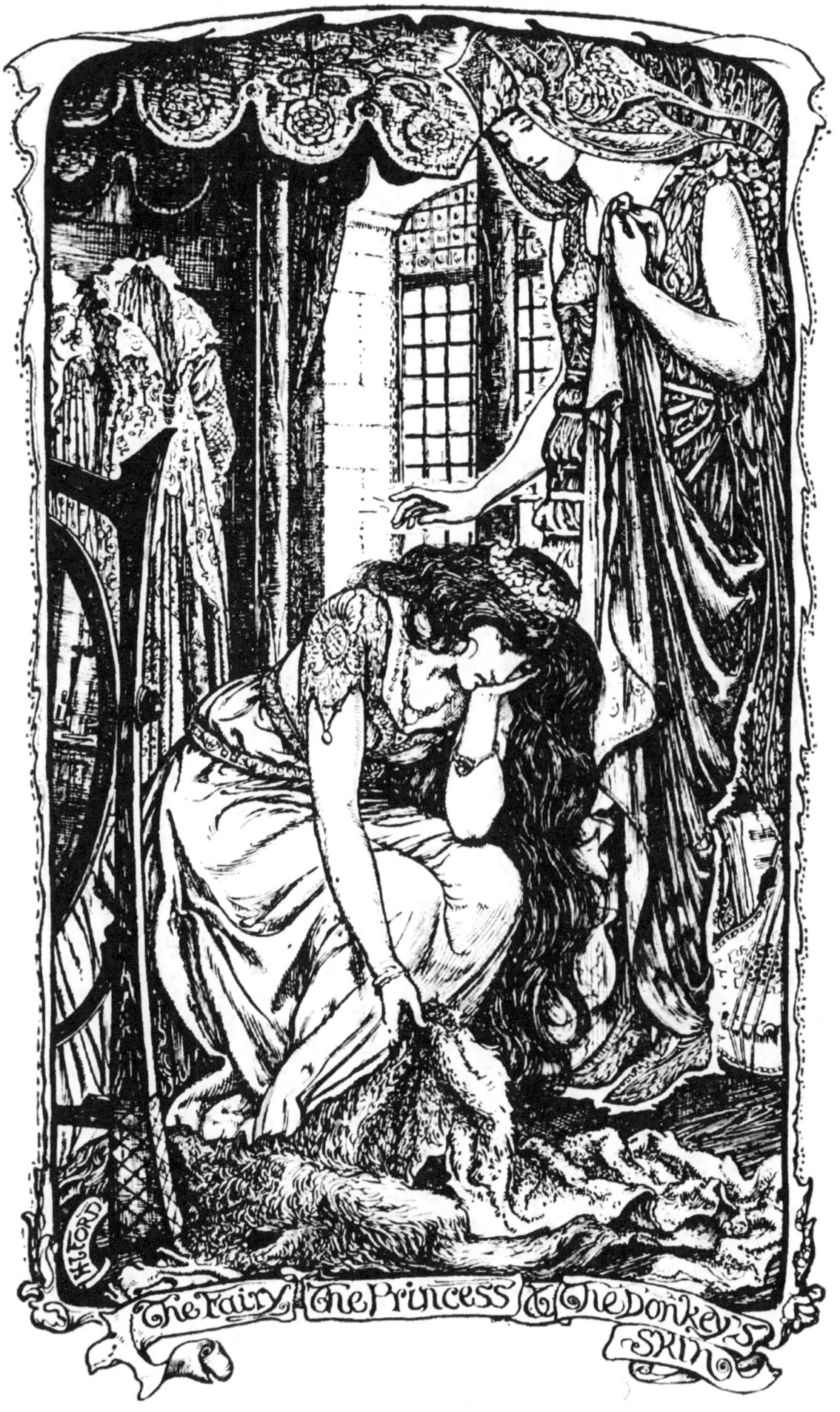

The Fairy, the Princess & the Donkey's Skin

Name:
Date:
Notes:

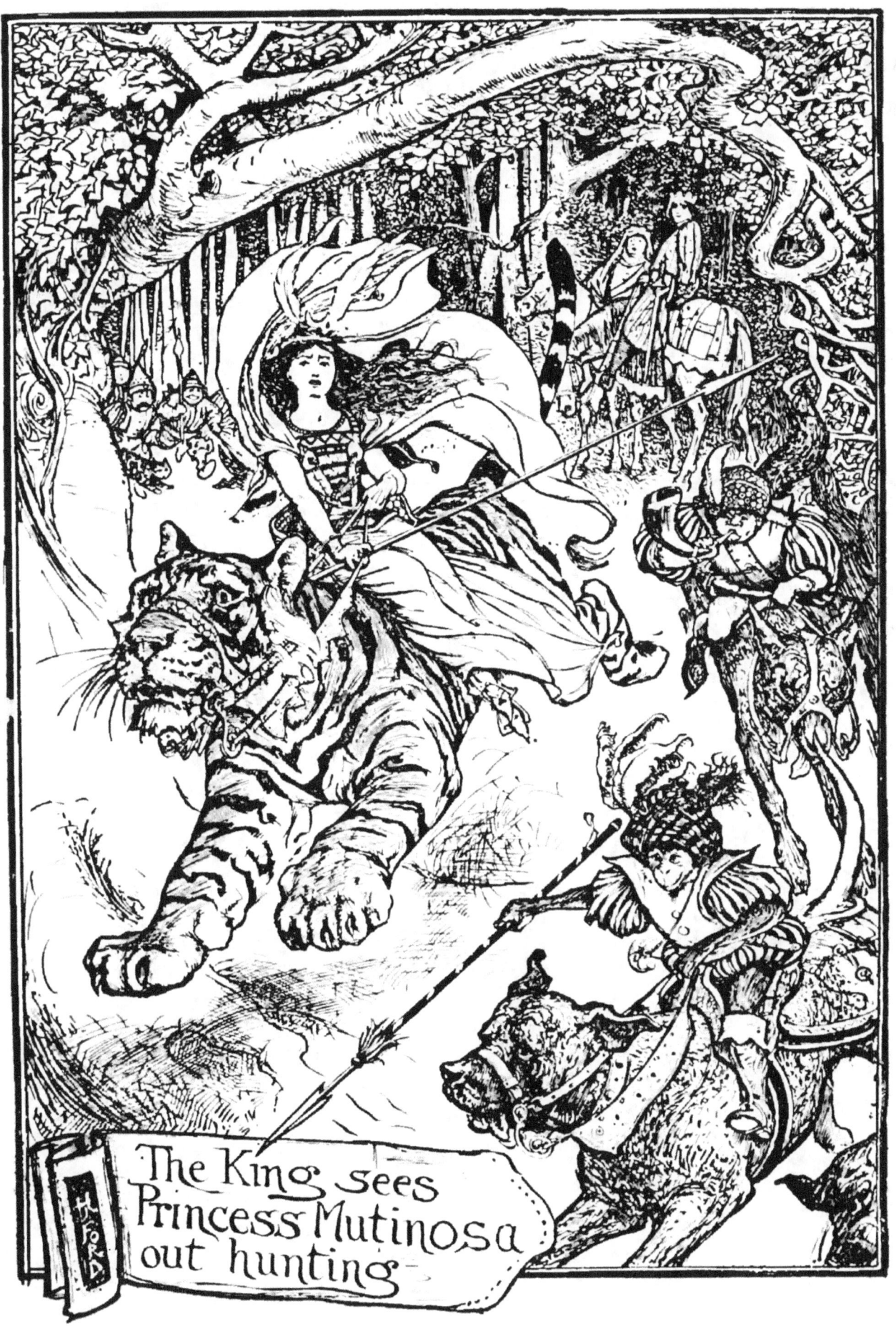

The King sees Princess Mutinosa out hunting

Name:
Date:
Notes:

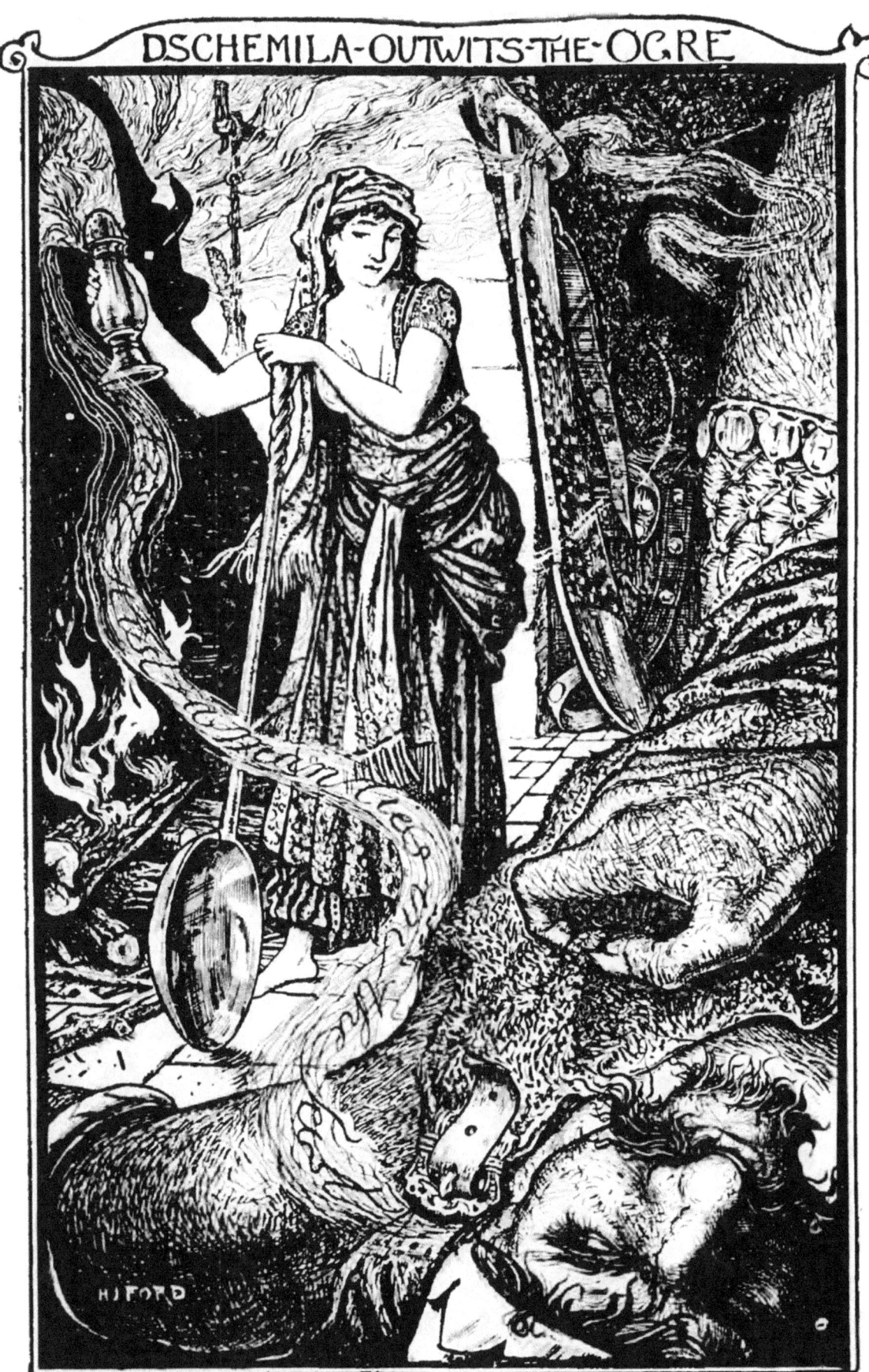

Name:
Date:
Notes:

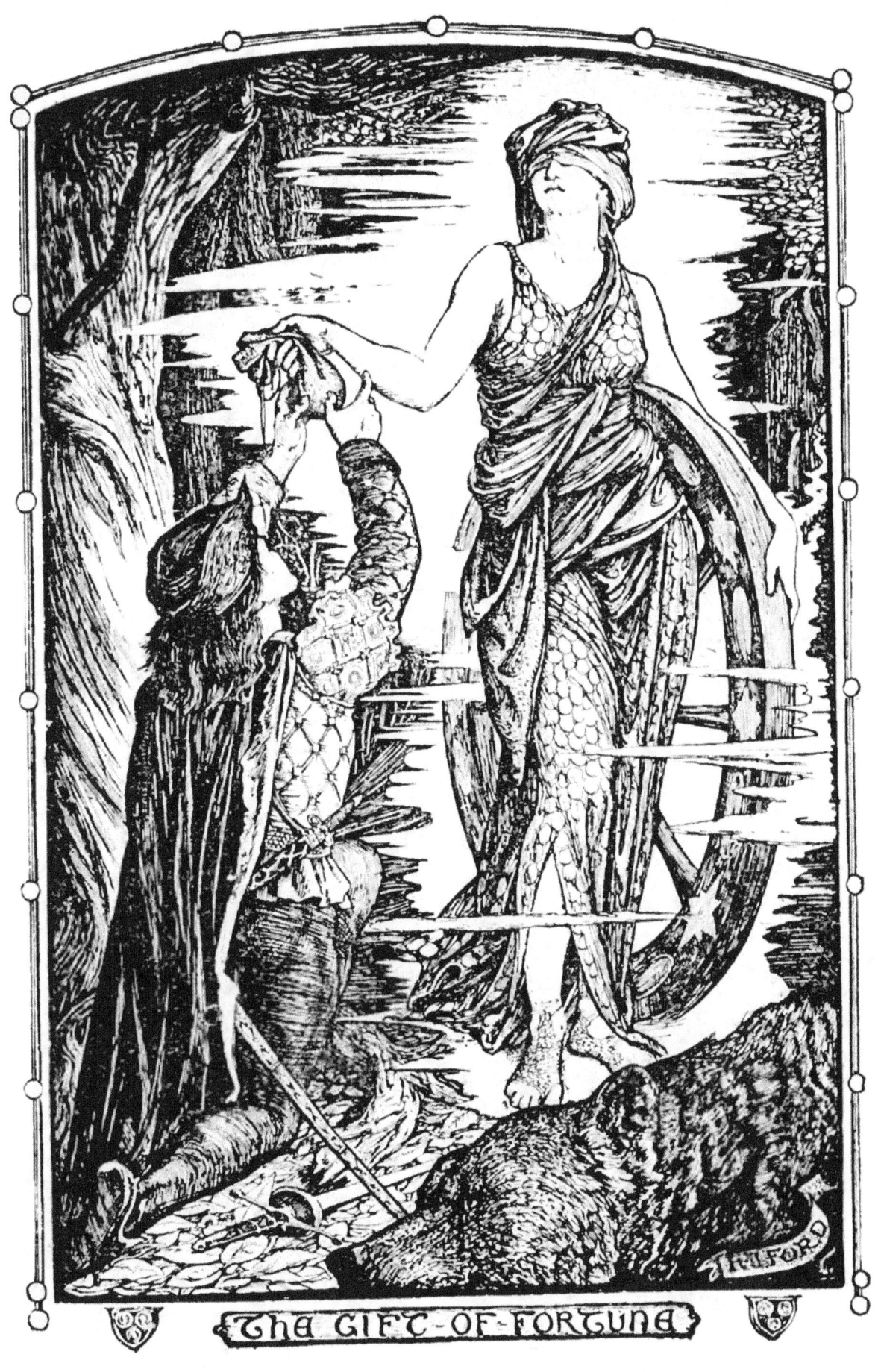

THE GIFT OF FORTUNE

Name:
Date:
Notes:

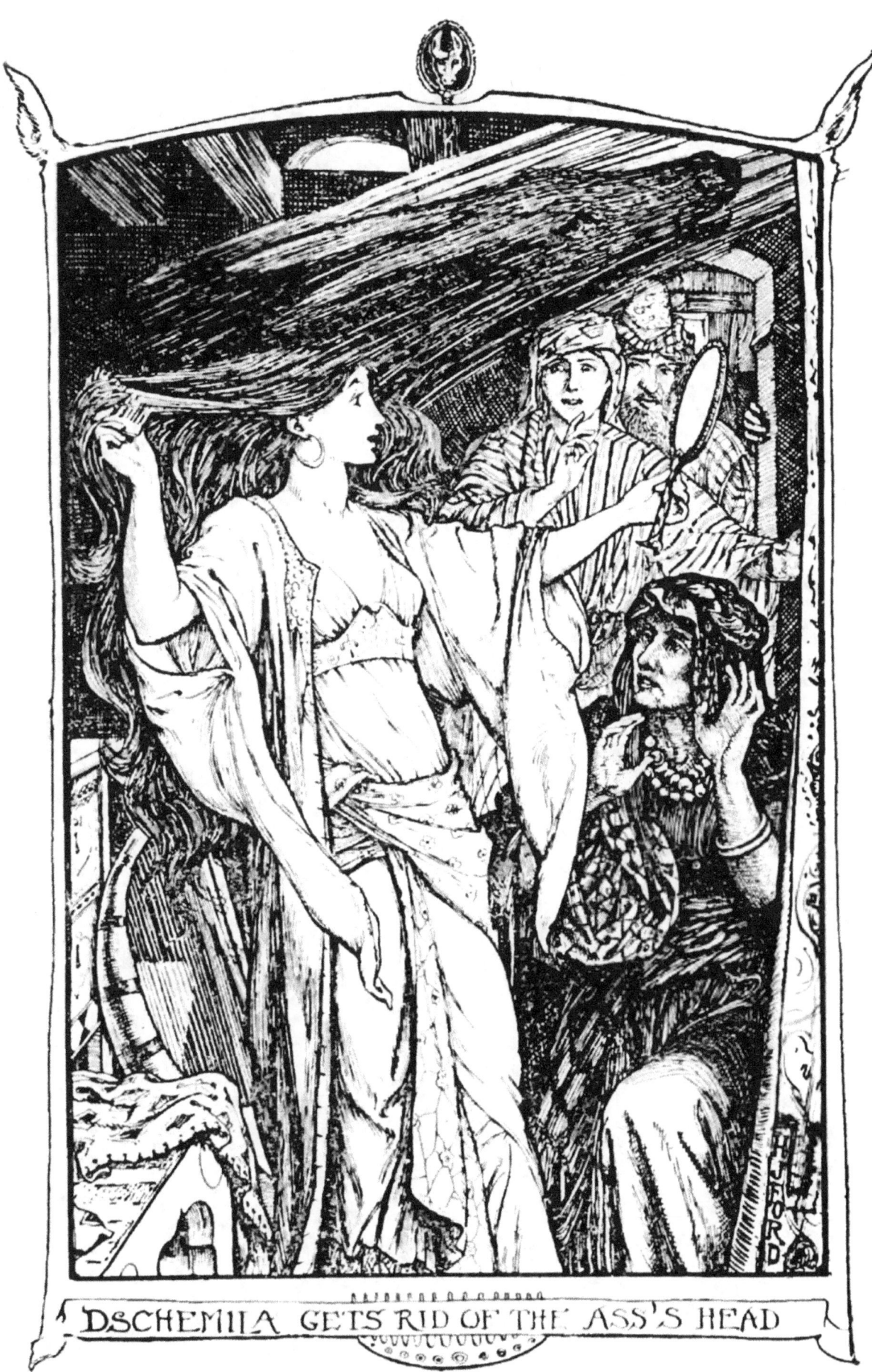

DSCHEMIIA GETS RID OF THE ASS'S HEAD

Name:
Date:
Notes:

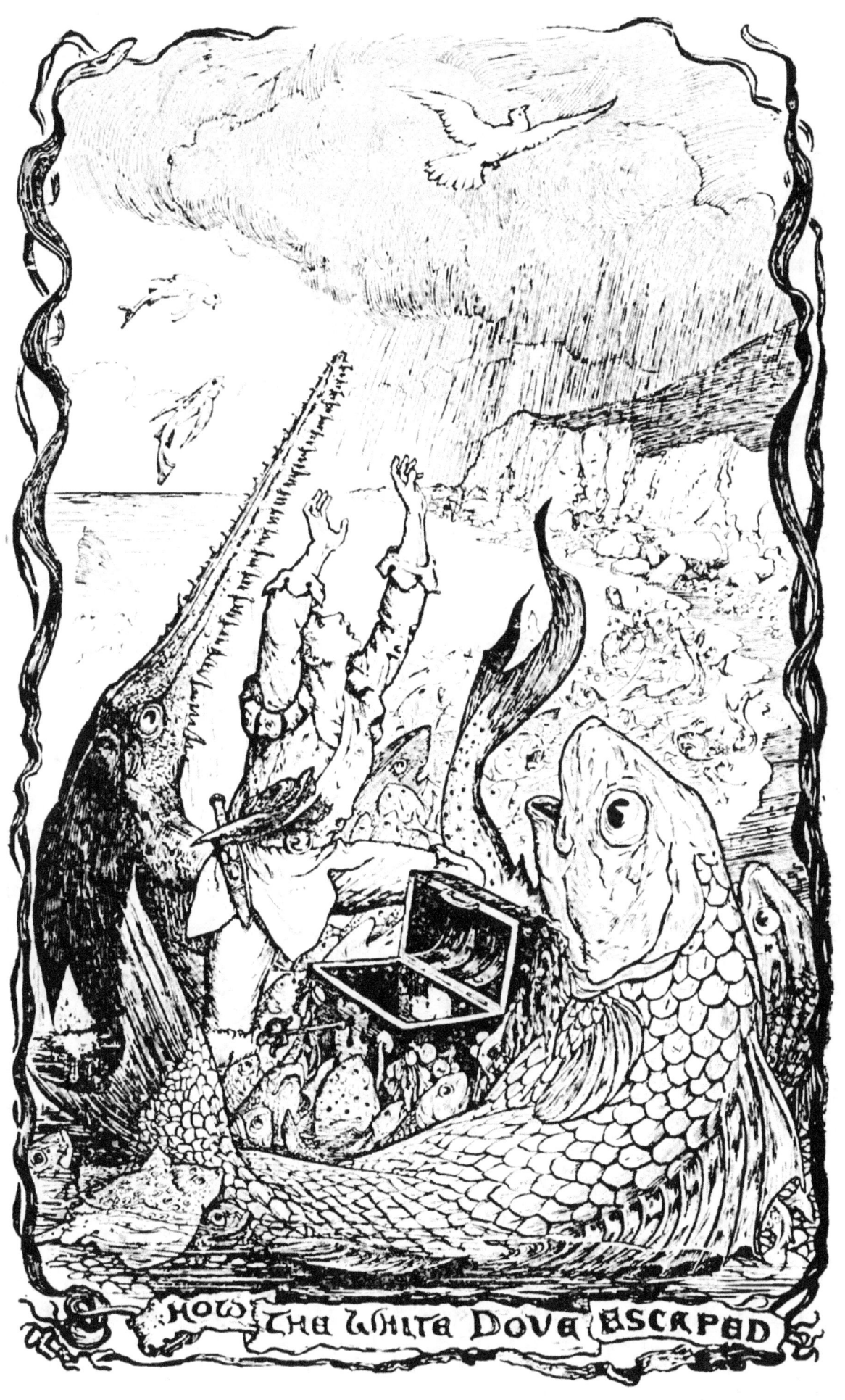

HOW THE WHITE DOVE ESCAPED

Name:
Date:
Notes:

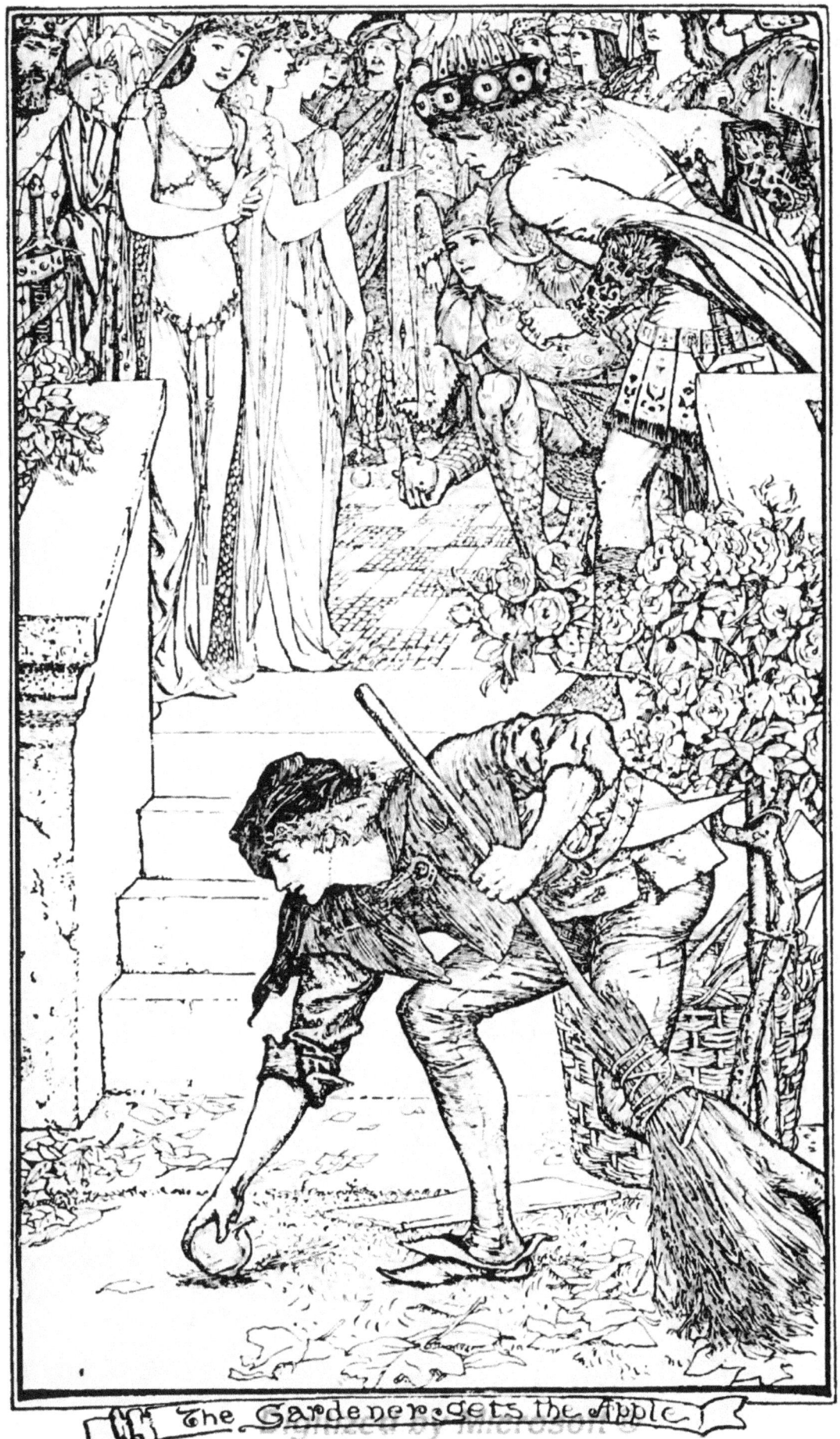

The Gardener gets the Apple

Name:
Date:
Notes:

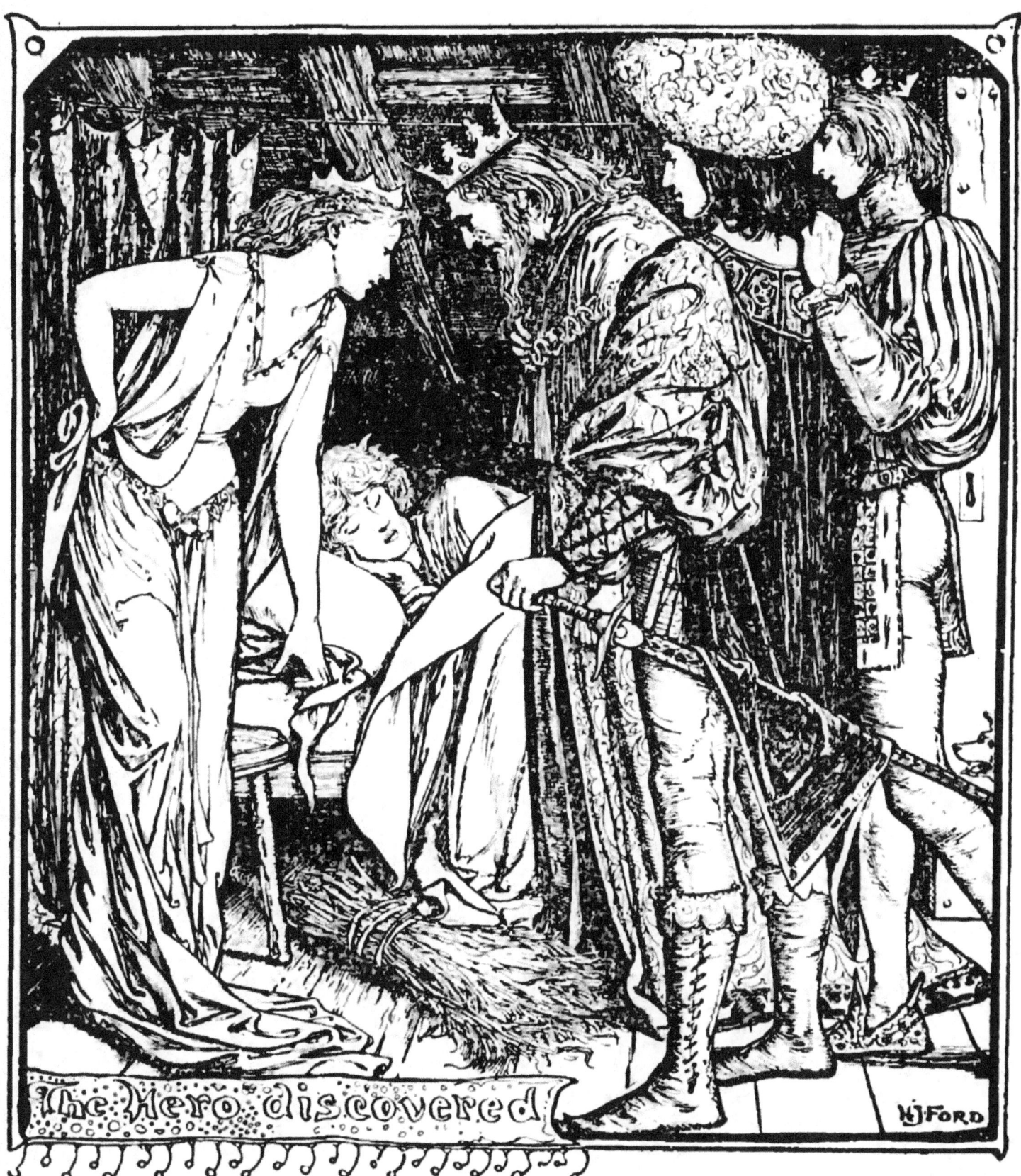

The Hero discovered

Name:
Date:
Notes:

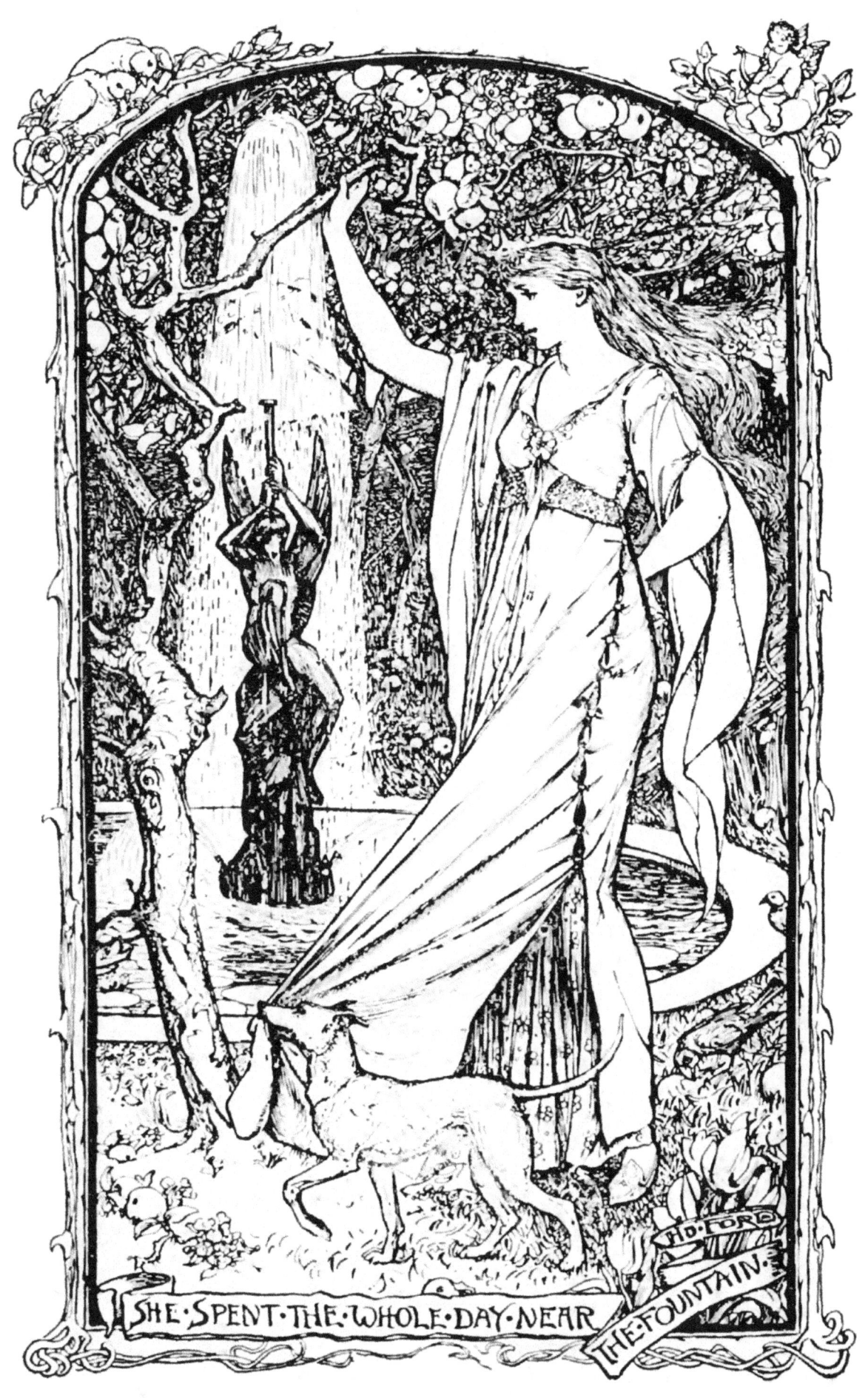

SHE·SPENT·THE·WHOLE·DAY·NEAR·THE·FOUNTAIN·

Name:
Date:
Notes:

Hawaiian Heritage Press

Hawai`i's finest classic and modern literature.

HawaiianHeritage.org

Sign up to learn about events, promotions and new releases

bit.ly/HawaiianHeritage

Images courtesy of archive.org and the Boston Public Library